"Garrett Kah... transparent wi... perspective and you can see ... in making something that impacts the kingdom rather than a social media following. Read this book and get yourself in a posture to look realistically at your relationship with Christ."

Tre' Giles
Youth Director - Celebration Community Church

"Throughout our day, we seem to be lost in social media/internet, in meaningless relationships as well piecing moments together that only last for hours of satisfaction. As human beings, we desire relationships that brings hope, love, joy and grace. We go out of our way to find the best relationship and end up empty. But we forget one thing: God desires relationship with us.

God's design in relationship with Him allows us to recognize that we aren't alone in this world. That the promises He has for us is more than earthly desires, but a burning desire of eternal relationship. Garrett gives the you the opportunity to experience God's intimacy and to accept the invitation of God's heart for you. God's been waiting for your "YES", it is time to walk with Him in His #Relationshipgoals for you!"

Damion Cooper
Youth Director and Pastor - GracePointe Community Church

PRAISE FOR #RELATIONSHIPGOALS

"There is no greater quest on the planet than knowing Christ! Garrett Kahrs not only writes about this in his book #Relationshipgoals, but he is one of the few who lives it. His contagious fire for Christ is bound to inspire you as he guides you on a journey of deepening your relationship with God."

Caleb Bislow
Author: Dangerous: Engaging the People and Places No One Else Will
Founder of Unusual Soldiers - Forge Itinerant Speaker

"Authentic personal experience has armed and equipped Garrett Kahrs with insight and passion for passing on to others what's radically transformed his own life - an intimate up-close RELATIONSHIP with God! It's not only what Jesus said, "matters most" in life - it's what he died for YOU to enjoy and experience!"

Dwight Robertson
Author: "You are God's Plan A", "Forged by Fire", "Is God Waiting for a Date with You?"
Forge Founding President & CEO

"This is not another book to read lounging around drinking coffee. This is a challenging and thought-provoking book that helps examine how Jesus wants to restore, support, and strengthen us through relationship."

Kevin Brown
Student Ministry Pastor - Grabill Missionary Church

"What a great way to look at how we connect with Jesus! #Relationshipgoals give a fresh perspective on the often mentioned, and even more often confusing, concept of having a relationship with Jesus. With a robust mix of Biblical illustrations and real life transparency, Garrett illustrates a path to relationship with Jesus that allows people to transcend the "motions" of religious practice."

Mike Crain
Lead Consultant - Ministry Architects

"I love that Garrett invested such a vast amount of time to write about friendship with Jesus! Even more, I love that he's been exploring friendship with Jesus personally!"

Dave Powers
Singer/Songwriter - Mountain City Music

#RELATIONSHIPGOALS

DISCOVERING GOD'S DESIRE AND DESIGN
FOR A RELATIONSHIP WITH HIM

GARRETT KAHRS

Unless noted otherwise noted, all Scripture taken from the HOLY BIBLE, NEW INTERNATIONAL VERSION®. NIV®. Copyright © 1973, 1978, 1984 by International Bible Society. Used by permission of Zondervan. All rights reserved worldwide.

Scripture quotations marked (NLT) are taken from the Holy Bible, New Living Translation, copyright ©1996, 2004, 2015 by Tyndale House Foundation. Used by permission of Tyndale House Publishers, Inc., Carol Stream, Illinois 60188. All rights reserved

KJV are taken from the the King James Version of the Bible. (Public Domain.)

ISBN: 0-692-15332-2

ISBN - 13: 978-0-692-15332-1

To my best friend, Talia.
Thank you for being an amazing woman of God!

CONTENTS

INTRODUCTION

My phone vibrated with an incoming text; its faint buzzing noise woke me from a deep sleep. I rolled over to grab it and saw a photo my wife had sent. She was in Nebraska spending a few days on a lake with her family. I opened the text with a grin to see a happy lake picture of her cousin, Kort, wake-surfing with his girlfriend on his shoulders. Duly impressed with this feat, I soon realized that my wife was not only sharing, but suggesting that we attempt the same with her. The next text was simply, #relationshipgoals.

I replied, telling her there was no way in the world I could pull that off. I could barely wake surf as it was, let alone put anyone on my shoulders. Through our texts, we laughed together over the idea. We both understood that I am terrible at most activities related to water sports and wouldn't be able to accomplish it.

However, this text from my wife sparked something new and unknown inside my heart. It was something that pointed me toward my relationship with God. It was soon after that text message that I began to realize how God described his desire for a relationship with me throughout scripture. This text kept me up that night until early the next morning. I began to search scripture and found that it is full of God describing his desire to be in a relationship with us. The bible was coming alive to me in a fresh way, and it was changing me.

I felt overwhelmed by a profound sense that God has relationship goals for me. With me.

I had always known that God loved me, but I didn't always act like it. I grew up in the church. My mom was a worship leader. I had given my life to Christ at a young age and even felt called to full-time vocational ministry in the 5th grade. Despite all of this, I hadn't fully understood the depth of his desire for relationship.

In all his infinite wisdom, God began to provide me with a picture of the relationship that he so desired to have with me. This moment was the beginning, the birth really, of not only this book, but of my journey into a deeper and more fulfilling relationship with Christ.

During my journey into the relationship that God desires, I realized that not only does God desire a deep relationship, but that he has a definite and specific design to that relationship. Slowly, he began to reveal his process for a journey with him.

We all serve a God who is the master designer. The beauty of his design continually surrounds us. Everything God created is filled with the genius of his intention and work. The same goes for our relationship with him.

I now know that discovering God's design and desire isn't something that will happen overnight, nor does it come instantaneously or effortlessly. Our culture has created a misguided belief that we can have everything we want or need, here and now, right at our fingertips. We have become an "instantaneous" generation of wanters, desiring everything quicker, easier, faster, newer, and better.

Stop for a moment to wonder how this belief affects our relationship with God.

We may want the benefits of knowing Christ without doing what it takes to develop a deeper level of intimacy with him. We cannot have in a moment what takes a lifetime to grow and develop. We cannot develop traits of intimacy overnight. There are few shortcuts in life, but there are no shortcuts to developing a better relationship with God. I'm here to say that if you thought by reading this book you would find those instant answers, you will be genuinely and sadly disappointed.

> "The worst thing a book can do for a Christian is to leave him with the impression that he has received from it anything good; the best it can do is to point the way to the Good he is seeking. The function of a good book is to stand like a signpost directing the reader toward the Truth and the Life.
>
> That book serves best which early makes itself unnecessary, just as a signpost serves best after it is forgotten, after the traveler has arrived safely at his desired haven. The work of a good book is to incite the reader to moral action, to turn his eyes toward God and urge him forward."[1]

In the chapters to follow, I will invite you into my story and the journey I followed towards God's desire and design for a relationship.

This book took years to write. While I wasn't writing on

my computer, I felt God writing it in my heart. I hope and pray that through reading these words, you would say yes to the journey God has for you and your own, unique relationship with him.

My prayer as you begin to read, is that you would open your eyes to see God's love in a new and powerful way! May you witness God's desire and design come alive in your relationship with him.

1

GOD'S DESIRE

Something was missing in my life. I searched for years to find out what it was. I believed that I could fill that void with sports, relationships, or even work. Those worldly 'fillers' lasted, but only temporarily, leaving space after the immediate rush for the empty feeling to return.

My life had become an endless search for satisfaction, meaning, belonging, and love.

In college, I thought I'd found that missing piece. I had great friends. I was in a 'good' relationship. I was a leader at my university in several different student organizations. People wanted to be around me, chose to be.

Being popular fed my quest for meaning yet in all the wrong ways. To be popular at my University, I thought I had to be involved in one avenue: attending and throwing parties. Three to four nights a week, I partied and partied hard. I often got so drunk that in the morning when I woke up, I couldn't remember what had happened the previous night. I loved to put on parties where hundreds of people attended, mostly with the intent of having people know me and like me. I thought that I had found what was missing from my life.

Everything in life seemed right.

Perhaps, almost perfect.

Then something happened, a moment that changed everything including the trajectory of my life's path. I became sick. At first, my symptoms had all the attributes of a simple, common cold. However, a few weeks into the illness, I began to believe that it was more than just a cold. I saw several different doctors to address the issue, hoping they would discover what was wrong.

The first doctor also thought I had a minor cold and prescribed vitamin C and rest. The second thought I pulled a muscle in my back. The diagnoses were as varied as the faces who delivered them, but no one could figure out what was wrong, and my symptoms continued to worsen.

I then began to have night sweats. I would wake up with extreme back and stomach pain. Sores had developed in my mouth, snaking their way down into the pit of my stomach. At one point, because of the sores, all I could manage to keep down without becoming ill was a bottle of Gatorade.

Days turned into weeks and weeks became months. Doctor after doctor attempted to determine my illness but couldn't diagnose the problem.

Finally, a doctor in Nebraska took the time to ask me some specific questions. It was my responses that led him to understand what was ultimately wrong.

As with the others, I initially lied to him about the amount of alcohol I'd been drinking, unwilling to reveal the truth. The papers in his hand that showed my blood test results had all the information he needed to catch me in the act, and he saw through my lies.

He asked me, "Son, I know what's wrong. Do you want the good news or the bad news first?"

I asked him to deliver the bad news, and he proceeded to tell me that at twenty-one years old, my liver was failing. He added that if I wanted to live longer, I would have to stop consuming alcohol altogether.

Hearing that prognosis at the age of 21 was the worst news I had ever received. I remember the room began to spin. I became extremely pale and lightheaded. The world seemed as if it had stopped.

Of all the possible problems that my body was experiencing, hearing that my liver was failing was the last problem I would have guessed. Despite my unhealthy appetite for alcohol and extended nights of drinking to excess, I still couldn't understand how this could happen to me.

Then I remembered the doctor suggested there was 'good news' in his delivery, and I wondered what that could possibly be.

He proceeded to tell me that he had diagnosed me correctly and caught the problem in time enough for my liver to heal. He explained that the liver organ has the capability of restoring itself, regenerating healthy cells. There, I learned more about the liver than I'd ever imagined knowing. The liver has an amazing ability to 'return' to its original function, even after it's been wrongly damaged.

For my liver to accomplish this feat, however, I could no longer consume alcohol and allow it to run through my body. In a few short years, my liver had handled more alcohol than most people would drink in a lifetime. By that point, it had become poison to my body just as my lifestyle had become poison to my soul.

Because I did not want to die, I made the decision to quit drinking then and there. This choice caused the life that I had lived before to nearly instantaneously crumble around me.

Back in school, the people who I'd thought were my best friends quickly moved on without a thought about my situation. Despite the years and time we'd spent together, it was as if no one cared. There were even times when those once-were-friends would actually make fun of my new decision not to drink.

The life I had built was destroyed.

I was undeniably lost.

In Luke 15, as Jesus sat amongst people who questioned his company, he began telling parables about things that were lost. He told a story of a wandering sheep who left behind the entire herd. Then, he shared a story about a missing coin that is extremely valuable to a woman who couldn't seem to find it. Finally, in the last story, he told of a lost son who loses everything.

Jesus contrasts the first two stories with the last one to make a point about who he is. In the first story, he told about a shepherd that goes looking for his missing sheep. The shepherd left ninety-nine sheep in the field to go find the one sheep that was lost.

In the second story, we see a woman frantically searching for the coin that she'd lost. Flipping her house upside down and inside out. Looking in every crack and crevice for where it might have been.

However, in the last parable, when the son leaves his home and lives a life of wild living, no one goes out in search of him.

We see in all these parables that God has the heart for the lost. He desires to restore people who have been misplaced, overlooked, wandered off, and even those who have squandered everything. Jesus, himself, is the shepherd, searching for the wandering sheep. He seeks out people who are valuable to him, more valuable than a sheep or a coin.

Not only does God come looking for us, but when he finds us, he throws a celebration for what was once lost has now been found.

Just as with the first two parables, Jesus came and found me.

I wasn't searching for him because I thought I already had him. Knew him. But he found me and understood that I needed to be found. In the midst of my struggles, I encountered the open arms of God in a way that would forever change me.

I believe that if you are lost, Jesus is on a search to find you. Despite our brokenness and inability to find God on our own, he sent his son on a mission to find us.[2]

Jesus came to earth to repair the relationship that was broken between humanity and himself. That's why he died on the cross. It's why he was raised from the dead three days later.

He is on a mission to find what is lost, and he has invited us all into a relationship with him.

Chosen

I believe that many people desire to restore a relationship with God, but it may be a misguided belief that God won't accept them that keeps them from this relationship.

When my life fell apart, at first I didn't believe that God would accept me back. I had done too many bad things. I had sinned too much.

Even though I had a relationship with him in my youth, I

thought there could be no way after I'd rebelled from him that he would allow me back into a relationship.

Through my struggles, I began to understand that I believed my rebellion against God to be higher than his redemption. I thought that because I had rejected him, he would, in turn, reject me back. However, as I encountered God's love for me, I learned that my rebellion and rejection of God would not revoke his reconciliation of my relationship with him.

I had a deep fear of rejection because of my deeper desire to be chosen. Being chosen gives us a sense of love and security. My fear of not being loved and accepted came from many years of being rejected by so many different people, particularly at my greatest time of crisis. This history of rejection made me believe that I was 'unlovable.' Moreover, when I'd finally found people who I thought cared about me in college, once I left the lifestyle we'd shared, they, in turn, left me and my wounds deepened.

The truth is that Jesus has never rejected us, no matter what we've done. In fact, even in the midst of rebelling from him, he demonstrated his never-ending love by his actions on the cross.[3]

When I began to encounter God's love, it changed everything. I learned that before I even knew of God's love, he died on the cross for you and me. In love, he chose to die to restore a relationship with us.

The truth is that his plan for a relationship with you did not begin today. God chose us before we were even walking on this Earth. God's plan for a relationship with you is as old as time itself. This is good news for us – for nothing will get in God's way of developing an intimate relationship with him!

God's choosing us, and he continues to choose us every

day. His undying love reminds me of the first time I told my wife that I loved her.

Before diving into the details of the story, however, I must share the part of the story that Talia so loves to tell. You see, when we began our relationship, I had created a few 'rules' for us to follow. The first rule was that we were not going to say I love you to one other until we were engaged. The second rule was that we were not going to kiss until our wedding day.

Well, just a few weeks into our relationship, I was the one who broke Rule Number One.

My 'lapse' happened when we were sitting in her car after her college basketball game, talking through the plays of the game. As I was leaving, without thinking twice as if it was the most natural thing in the world, I told her I loved her. As I waited for what seemed like an eternity, the awkward silence was deafening. She was not about to break the rule that I, myself, had set in place weeks before.

You see, I couldn't help but break my rule! I was already crazy in love with this woman, and I had to let her know how I felt. In fact, before she even knew of me, I'd already spent several months in prayer about pursuing a relationship with her.

God has done the same with our relationship. Well before we ever enter into a relationship with him, he was saying 'I love you' through his actions on the cross.

God has never rejected us.

He has chosen us.

If you believe that God has chosen you, then I want you to write your name in this blank.

_____ , I choose you. Despite your past or any of your failures, I choose you. Nothing can keep me from choosing you. The deepest desire that I have is to be in a relationship with you.

Now let these words sink into the depths of your heart. It almost seems unfathomable, but God's deepest desire is to be in a relationship with us.

Take a moment to ask yourself, what is keeping you from a healthy, relationship with God?

Maybe you are like me and believe you could never be accepted back into a relationship with him. Or perhaps you think that you have to somehow 'get better' and make things right before God will allow you back.

God knew we would rebel from a relationship with him. Yet, he still chose to not only create us, but also create a way for our relationship with him to be restored. God has implanted the sincere desire for us to be chosen in our hearts. He genuinely wants us to come to him, and to choose him, in return.

The radical part of the gospel is that Jesus died for people who he knew would never choose to have a relationship with him. Despite God choosing us and paving a way towards a relationship with him, he has still given us the right to respond to his invitation and choose him in return. Our ability to choose him has come from a God who has chosen us.

For the record, Talia did respond to me after I told her I loved her. Just not until the next day. After the surprise and shock of my admission had passed, she told me that she loved me, too.

What will your response be to God's love towards you?

Desire

As I began a new relationship with Christ, I found the answer to what seemed to be missing for so many years. The answer was simple, intimacy with God. We are created for an intimate relationship that fulfills our desire to be known and loved. Each of us has an innate desire for that relationship. We all crave a sincere, authentic, thriving connection. Some have found this in relationships with the people around us, but for many of us, most of our relationships on this Earth have fallen flat of our desire for real and fulfilling intimacy.

C. S. Lewis speaks of desires that can never be fulfilled in his book, *Mere Christianity*. He writes:

> "If I find in myself a desire which no experience in this world can satisfy, the most probable explanation is that I was made for another world. If none of my earthly pleasures satisfy it, that does not prove that the universe is a fraud. Probably earthly pleasures were never meant to satisfy it, but only to arouse it, to suggest the real thing."

This world, and our desire to be in a relationship within it, only offer us a small glimpse of the ultimate relationship for which we were created. While we may achieve momentary satisfaction in our relationships here on Earth, we will never achieve eternal satisfaction outside of a relationship with Christ. God uses the connections that we have in this world to arouse our desire for a relationship with him. Unsatisfied desires for a deeper relationship will always leave us wanting for something more.

That something more is a relationship with God.

God's desire to have a relationship with his creation has always been his central goal. He created us to be in close relationship with him. The first human beings, Adam and Eve, walked with God in the Garden of Eden at the beginning of time. Both God's plan and purpose have been centered around being together with his people. From the Garden to the tabernacle, the temple, Jesus, the Holy Spirit, and eternity, God's desire has always been to be with his people.

God has designed not only our life on this world but eternity around a relationship with him. Despite sin coming into the world and causing us to be separated from God's original design for our lives, we see at the end of time that God will restore all things. Only then will his people truly walk with him again![4]

Throughout scripture, we see God's desire for relationship popping out from the pages. One of the countless stories in the Bible that gives us insight into God's desire for relationship is in the story of Enoch. Enoch's story is tucked away within three verses in Genesis. His life is so worthwhile that the writer of Genesis highlighted Enoch's life and took the time to mention his specific story in Genesis 5.

> *"After he became the father of Methuselah,*
> *Enoch walked faithfully with God 300*
> *years and had other sons and daughters.*
> *Altogether, Enoch lived a total of 365*
> *years. Enoch walked faithfully with God;*
> *then he was no more, because God took*
> *him away.* "[5]

Enoch's faith and life with God was so breathtaking that even another writer mentions him in Hebrews 11.

> *"By faith Enoch was taken from this life, so*
> *that he did not experience death: He could*

not be found, because God had taken him
away. For before he was taken, he was
commended as one who pleased God."[6]

Even though we do not know that much about Enoch, we do know that he walked with God for nearly four of our life-times. Enoch spent his life on this earth walking with and beside God. He fully understood God's desire to walk inti-mately with his people.

God wants more than just a momentary experience with each and every one of us. He wants to spend eternity with us. God's desire doesn't only mean something to us right now, on this Earth, but it has eternal implications, as well.

Relationship Goals

God's desire doesn't end with our response to his invitation to a relationship. In fact, that invitation is just the beginning. He wants us to continue to grow in our intimacy with him as we live out our days on this Earth.

As I continued to develop in my intimacy with God, he began to show me through scripture that he describes exactly what he wants our relationship with him to look like.

God described his desire for my relationship with him similarly to a social media hashtag. This hashtag was #rela-tionshipgoals. #Relationshipgoals is used by people online who use a picture or some text to describe their desire for relationship. Millions of people worldwide use this hashtag to post their wants and desires for a relationship.

When God began to show me his relationship goals for me, it was like sending a picture of his desire for our rela-tionship.

In the beginning, it was difficult for me to fathom the

depth of the relationship that he wanted me to walk in. Slowly, he began to show me through John 15 what his invitation to friendship would look like. Later, I found in Ephesians 5 that I am the Bride of Christ, pointing to his promise about the strength and depth of our relationship. He then showed me that all of his promises are for me and are intended to build a deeper relationship with him. His invitations into a deeper relationship continued as I found them in Scripture.

Many times, when I was shown his desire, it looked different than the relationship I'd previously had with him. When he showed me I was his friend, I had no clue what a friendship with him would be like. When he told me I was his child, that he'd adopted me and he was my Father, I was shell-shocked.

I didn't know how to be God's friend.

I definitely didn't know how to be his child.

When he shared these details with me, it wasn't to condemn me for not knowing them, or not being in the place where I should be with him. They were simply part of Jesus' invitation into his desire for our relationship together.

God's relationship goals take us to a newfound depth in our relationship with him. While I discovered his desire, I spent hours asking him what that meant. What it meant to him to be friends. What it means to be his child. How I should walk as his bride on Earth.

Now, not only do I know that Jesus is my friend, we are great friends. Best of friends, really. He is my father, and I am his adopted child. And my journey in our relationship hasn't ended.

It is only the beginning.

God shares his desire for what our relationship with him could and should look like through scripture. God's Word is full of his invitations. Just as he invited me into his desire for relationship, he invites you, as well.

We will look into some of these relationship goals in the second half of this book. Although you may want to skip ahead, I would encourage you to read the next few chapters first. These chapters will help set a foundation for us to continue to develop intimacy with God.

2

GOD'S DESIGN

God's design and desire for our relationship go hand-in-hand. To walk in his desire, we must follow his design. Our relationship with God will never be in a place where we desire it to be without his design. God doesn't leave us to fend for ourselves after calling us into a relationship with him. He walks alongside us, giving us the steps we need to achieve his design for our relationship.

As God rescued me from my own series of wrong turns, I began by asking myself what God's design for my relationship with him would be. Unsure of the answer to this question, I asked believers around me.

Many different answers and perspectives, along with a few blank stares came forth. Slowly, I began to realize some people just didn't know.

If I were to ask you, what is God's design for your relationship with him, what would you say?

For many years, I believed that what happened in my life was haphazard, purely by chance or circumstance. That there was no structure, no plan. I was trying to follow God the best that I knew how, and hoping it would all turn out all right.

God showed me that he does have a plan. He had already thought through every step of my journey and well before I even knew about my quest for it. God can and will take each of us through different stages and reveal to us how to walk with him, in both the difficult times and the great times.

As I searched for his design for my life, I studied the Israelites' journey towards the promised land. God's plan for the Israelites' journey was almost tangible to me as I read it in Scripture. This is where God's design for my relationship with him began to come alive. I found myself in seasons of trusting God and walking with him similarly to them. While I wasn't in the middle of a desert, I learned that God would help me walk with him in different stages in his design for my life.

The Israelites' journey took years; decades, in fact. God didn't merely rescue them and leave them to figure out their lives on their own. He walked with them through the desert. God was there when they ran out of water and needed to drink. He was there when they were hungry. He rained down mana from heaven and provided water, guiding them with his presence and showing them how to walk with him.

Similarly to the Israelites being led by the pillar of cloud and fire, God helps us on our journey through the work of the Holy Spirit.[7] He will go alongside us as we continue to walk in God's design for our lives. He will comfort us in difficult seasons. He will develop trust in the journey we are on, and he will help us walk into the destiny we are created for.

Just as with the Israelites, we can discover God's design and plan for our journey with him.

Stages

God accomplishes his design through stages or what some refer to as seasons. In Ecclesiastes, the author begins chapter three by discussing the many different seasons of life we face. He tells us that there is a season for everything and every activity on Earth. There is a time to be born and a time to die. A time to plant and a time to uproot. A time to kill and a time to heal. Time to tear down and build. Weep and laugh. Mourn. Dance. Embrace. Search. Give up. Love and hate. To have war and to have peace.[8]

The author is inviting us into an understanding that everything that we will face in our lifetime has a design. Even when we face seasons that seem pointless, God has a plan for what we walk through in our lives.

We get to look into the different stages in God's plan for the Israelites journey in Numbers 33. At the beginning of this chapter, God asked Moses to record the stages they had been through. So Moses began recording them as he looked back in time and saw how God had accomplished his design through a series of different stages. We see through the journey of the Israelites that they walked through a variety of seasons in their journey to the promised land. We too will also walk through many different stages through our journey with God.

When we say yes to God's invitation, we need to understand that his design for our relationship is unique.

Not one person's journey will be the same.

This is both beautiful and amazing! It is like an original painting with no reproductions. The way God designed our very relationship, is distinct and unique for each of us. Custom-fit. Specialized. There is not another 'YOU' in this world, and your journey with God is as unique as you are.

You may find people who are in similar seasons or have had similar paths that you are on. However, God has so designed your journey with him that it is a place for only you to discover. The difficulty in our unique journeys is that we sometimes get caught up in comparison against others.

Why isn't my journey like my neighbor's?

Why does his or her life 'look' better?

Even more so, when we witness someone in a stage of their lives we want, or daresay covet, we may try to walk with God like them to achieve our desires. This incorrect thinking and unrealistic expectation often leads to discouragement.

No one else can be on your journey for you, just as you cannot follow another's marked journey. In the midst of our different stages, we must remember what the journey is all about. Being with God.

We see in Exodus 33 that Moses was more concerned about God's presence than he was about accomplishing what God had promised. They were so close to walking into the promised land God had given to them. When Moses spoke to God about the promise land, I was shocked by his words. Moses told God that if he didn't go with them into the next stage, he would not go either. Moses knew God's presence was more important to him and to Israel than trying to fulfill any promises without him.[9]

There will always be stages in our lives where we will face similar challenges and temptations. Times when we may attempt to make it more about the stage that we are in than about him. We can be so focused on our individual circumstances that we forget who is with us.

Our eyes are not on Jesus if they are only on ourselves, or even the journey that we are on. To accomplish God's design in our lives, we must keep our eyes on the only one who knows and created that design.

Difficult Stages

It took many years before I began to understand God's plan for me. During those years, I rebelled against my Christian faith, particularly during those times when I faced difficult circumstances.

I thought that as a Christian, everything should be okay. I believed I wouldn't have to deal with adversity if I obediently followed God. Part of my rebellion came from this misunderstanding. When I faced suffering, I couldn't understand why God allowed it in my life. There have been many moments when I believed there was no way God could do anything with the difficult circumstances that I faced.

Family members with Cancer.

Friends dying.

We all face seasons that seem impossible to walk through.

Look at the Israelites who lived in slavery for centuries before being rescued. Then when they were escaping Egypt, they became "trapped" by the Red Sea.[10] When they were walking in the desert there were times that they lived without a source of water. At one point on their journey to the promised land, they surely thought God had forsaken them.

We don't serve a God who cannot work through our impossible situations. God loves to show up in the midst of what we believe is impossible to show us that nothing is impossible with him. There will be many times during our relationship with God that also look more difficult than what you planned on. Just because you encounter difficulties doesn't mean you are in the wrong place.

As I have pastored college students in the past, one of the

themes that continues to creep up when students face difficult circumstances is that they immediately conclude that
something is wrong. Many times, they believe they have
made a wrong decision or even done something to
anger God.

While there certainly may be consequences for wrong
choices, such as what I faced with my physical health after
years of rebellion, there are times when we are not in the
wrong place, nor did we make a wrong decision. When we
face difficult situations, it might just mean that we are in the
exact place that God wants us to be.

Jesus didn't promise us that we would never face difficult
circumstances. Indeed, he told us that we would.[11] When we
go through difficult stages, our trust in God won't be shaken
or weakened if we hold onto his promises in the middle of
difficult circumstances.

He will be with us in the midst of grief and pain.

He will be by our sides during sorrow.

For the Lord promised us that he would never leave us or
forsake us.[12] He promises us that he is always faithful and
that we can trust him.

Difficult circumstances don't change who God is, and
they don't change his faithfulness or his promises to us. If
anything, difficult circumstances magnify his faithfulness and
his character.

As our Protector.

As our Provider.

And as our Comforter.

Trust

It is important to recognize that God often uses difficult and
changing circumstances to nurture and develop our trust in

him. If we never faced anything difficult, how would our trust in him grow?

God uses the earthly difficulties we face to grow us into the person whom he designed us to be.

God urges us to trust in his plan even when it does not make sense. His design for our walk with him is not always linear, clearly marked, or designed the way we believe it should be. In our world, $1 + 2 = 3$. Yet in God's design, it may look more like $X - U + Q \times 7 = A$.

In the journey of the Israelites, we learn that God wasn't leading them through the shortest route towards the promise land.[13] Why? Because God knew that if they were to encounter war that early on, they would turn back and return to Egypt. God was protecting and providing the best route for the Israelites. The way he led them took longer, and they knew this truth. However, if they would have taken the fastest route, they would have encountered enemies they were not prepared to face.

God isn't concerned about the fastest route for your life. He is more concerned about deepening our trust and our relationship with him. There will be many times on our journey that we do not, and cannot, fully comprehend the reason we are going through our current circumstance. God is working to shape the way you see circumstances through his eyes, and he is asking you for your trust in him.

We see God trying to develop a deep sense of the Israelites trust in his plan throughout the stages in their lives. They were led each day and night through the desert by a pillar of fire and clouds. God also provided just enough food for each day. God led the Israelites stage-by-stage, and day-by-day to develop their trust in him. As with most everything in life, we don't receive everything all at once. Most of the time, God's design for our lives happens one step at a time.

There will be times where we face a temptation to ask God for more than he is planning on giving us. We want clarity on our journey. We want to see what is further ahead, often ignoring what is right in front of us. Know that when God doesn't give us the entire process in one quick download, it is because he is building our trust in him. Every stage we are in allows for an increasing journey of commitment, love, and trust.

Even though there were times we see the Israelites trusting God, they struggled in the area of trust. Despite all that God did for the Israelites in the desert, it was the Israelites' distrust in God that led them to live another forty years in the desert.[14] If we can't trust God in the 'desert' stage of our life, then we won't be able to trust him in the promised land. It's essential for each of us to recognize that the stage we are in may actually be extended if we are unable to trust God in the deep places of our life.

God is always developing a higher level of trust in our lives. He does this because it is essential to developing a deeper level of intimacy with him. We can't grow in our intimacy with God without trusting him, and the depth of our trust will determine the level of intimacy each of us will have together with him.

In our lifetime, the most significant attack on our relationship with God will come at our trust in him. Our relationship with God will rip at the seams if that trust fades. We can't have a relationship with someone that we don't trust. Trust is essential to developing intimacy with God. Without it, we can't fulfill God's desire for a beautiful and fulfilling relationship.

Opposition

We will inevitably encounter resistance in our journey toward a deeper relationship with God. This happens because we have an enemy who will try to keep us from where we are headed. The enemy doesn't want you to grow or move into the places God has for you. Satan also doesn't want you to realize that you are walking in the fulfillment of what God has promised!

There were significant differences between the Israelite's time in the desert and the time in the promised land. One significant difference you will notice is the amount of resistance that the Israelites had in the promised land, compared to when they were living in the desert. While there are many difficulties in the desert, there isn't major opposition like we see in the promised land.

Just as we face difficult circumstances, when we encounter opposition it doesn't always mean that we have made a wrong choice or sinned against God. It may simply mean that we are exactly where God wants us to be.

The problem is that we face an enemy who does not want us to be in a close relationship with God. He will come at us with everything that he has to keep us away from the relationship God desires.

The enemy will never be satisfied until we are back, living in slavery to what held us captive before we knew Christ. However, if we will never go back to that slavery, our enemy will try to keep us in the desert stage, stopping us from walking into what God has promised us. The enemy hates fulfilled promises. He hates when believers are fully equipped and willing to fight against him.

Even though this enemy exists, we must not give him any

more credibility than he deserves. Too much talk about this enemy can give him more power than he should have.

God is all-powerful.

God is all-knowing.

God is entirely devoted to leading us to the destiny he has mapped out for us.

We will encounter fierce battles as we follow Christ. However, we must remember, on the other side of this opposition is a greater depth of relationship with God. In this midst of our battles, even when we don't see him there, God has not forsaken us.

He will fight the battle with us and for us.

Trust him and trust in his plan.

Change

Many times, as seasons change in our lives, the ways that God works in our lives will also change. As the Israelites walked into the promised land, the way they walked with God seemingly changed. He stopped leading them by the pillar of fire and a pillar of clouds. He also stopped providing them with their daily supply of manna once they crossed over into the promised land.

Our relationship with God will mature and grow in the midst of these different stages. God didn't change how he was showing up in the Israelite's life because he was mad or angry. It was merely a different stage of relationship with God, and therefore certain aspects of it also changed.

We cannot fall into frustration and doubt when this happens. When God provides a different way, that doesn't mean he isn't our provider any longer. When God leads us differently, he is still our leader. God is unchanging despite our ever-changing circumstances. When we encounter this change in relationship with God, it is a continuation of deepening our trust in him.

As our seasons change, will we believe that God is still our provider even though he is providing differently? Will we still believe God is our protector and deliverer? Will we still believe God is unchanging in the midst of our ever-changing circumstances?

Road Sick

There have been many times in my journey with God when I've become frustrated and wanted to quit. This happened because I would begin to focus on the destination of the journey rather than the process of reaching the destination.

A similar thing happened to me on my honeymoon with my wife, Talia. In the middle of our honeymoon in Maui, Hawaii, we decided to travel from one side of the island to the other. That day, our destination was Hāna, a small town on the east end of the Island. We'd been told how beautiful the trip would be, and that there were many destination spots to stop at, along the way.

The sheer beauty of the Hawaiian landscape was evident as soon as we left the hotel, heading east on the Road to Hāna. We used an online travel guide for this fantastic tour of Maui. The tour guide was a downloadable app that helped us navigate not only the road but also the entire trip. The guide alerted us to upcoming stops that would be worthwhile to explore. These stops included hikes, places to eat, waterfalls, and so much more. At these destinations, we could choose whether or not to stop and enjoy the beauty that was there, or go past and continue on.

As we began, Talia drove, and we started to get the hang of the curves the area is known for. Our guide told us that the road has approximately 620 curves, all due to the ocean as well as the island terrain.

On the journey, we were continually witnessing amazing waterfalls, sopping wet rainforests, aqua-blue ocean views, white sandy beaches, and bamboo forests. We even stopped to look at the now famous rock, featured in the first Jurassic Park movie.

Despite the beauty that surrounded us on all sides, eventually, the vast number of curves in the road made me very carsick. Nearly halfway through the journey, I was almost at the point of demanding Talia to pull over so I could relieve my upset stomach.

Because of this, we started to drive past more and more of those fantastic destination points, places we could have enjoyed had I not been ill. By that point, the Road to Hāna wasn't exactly a nightmare, but it had ceased to become the dream trip I'd envisioned for a honeymoon with my new wife.

Many of the stages that God gives is much like the Road to Hāna. There are many curves, one lane bridges as well as many amazing destinations along the way. It can be a beautiful journey if you take time to look around and see everything along the way. However, when we become sick of the journey, we end up missing its beauty, and we miss out on the many destinations that God has for us on the way.

Being sick of the journey can also cause us to want to quit and not continue down the path that God has designed for us. I have seen many believers, myself included, who are tired and worn out from the journey they have been on. Some have even given up on trying to get to the destination they believed God was calling them toward.

Where are you at in your journey with God? Are you to the point of being sick and tired of the process you are going through? I was only able to finish the trip to Hāna because of my wife's love and encouragement. We as believers need someone to help us on the journey we are on with God. We aren't meant to walk it alone.

If you are in a place in your journey with God where you don't want to continue any longer, let me encourage you. It is worth it. In fact, it is the only worthwhile journey on this earth. There is no better place to be than in God's unique design for your life!

THE STRUGGLE IS REAL

There are two main struggles that keep us from or cause us to struggle in a relationship with God. One of the struggles we face is sin. Simply defined, sin is rebellion against God and his commands. It is sin that caused a chasm between sinful humans and a perfect God. Thankfully, Jesus came to Earth to save us from our sin and from rebellion against him.

Another struggle we face is performance-based Christianity. Performance-based Christianity means trusting more in what we can do for God than what he has done for us. This happens when we erroneously place our trust in our own righteous works. A performance-based relationship is something that has infiltrated much of the church in today's time. Unfortunately, it has also infiltrated our other earthly relationships as well.

Developing a relationship with God is the most vital aspect of our Christian walk. In fact, it is finding intimacy with God that is the purpose of Christianity. Intimacy with God is often tricky. At times, it may seem as if we aren't growing in intimacy with God or that we feel a constant struggle in our walk with him. Both sin and performance-based Christianity cause various difficulties that come with our walk with God. However, Jesus came to rescue us from our sin, and from a performance-based relationship with him.

Sin

Our rebellion from God, starting with Adam and Eve, created a divide between our lives and him. Because of our rebellion, our lives are marked by being distant from him before coming into a relationship with God.

So what happened exactly? How did we end up this way? Turning to Genesis where this all began, will provide the answers. After the creation of Earth and everything in it, God commanded Adam that he must not eat from the tree of the knowledge of good and evil growing in the garden.[15] Out of the many trees in the Garden of Eden, there was just one tree that Adam was forbidden to eat from. Despite being told that eating from the tree would lead to death, we see both Adam and Eve rebelling against the command God gave them.

We also see in Genesis 3 that Satan in the form of a serpent was the cause of their decision. Satan did not want people to have an intimate relationship with God, nor does he still. In this passage, he went into the garden and attacked the relationship that God had created with humanity. The enemy convinced Adam and Eve that God was holding out on them and that their lives would be missing something if they didn't eat from the tree. This happened because the serpent specifically targeted the trust between God and his creation. The serpent in the garden questioned God's goodness in forbidding them to eat from the forbidden tree. Despite living in the perfect world, Adam and Eve were led to feel unsatisfied, and they fell for the devil's scheme.

In the thousands of years since that original sin, the

enemy has continued to bring into question God's goodness. When we question God's character, if he is actually good, we also begin to fall down that slippery slope, a slope which oftentimes leads to our sin against God.

Note that all such rebellion is not intentional. When we choose to sin, we do not do it because we know it will be destructive. Sins biggest deception is that many times when we face temptations, they appear as if it isn't rebellion against God, but instead it appears as if it is something good for us.

In Genesis 3, we see that Eve did not choose to eat from the tree of the knowledge of good and evil because she recognized that it was terrible for her.

> *"When the woman saw that the fruit of the tree*
> *was good for food and pleasing to the eye,*
> *and also desirable for gaining wisdom, she*
> *took it and ate it. She also gave some to*
> *her husband, who was with her, and he ate*
> *it."[16]*

She chose it because, at that time, it looked good. She was deceived, just as we sometimes are deceived by things that appear to be good for us.

This is the ultimate trick that sin plays on us. Sin will often disguise itself as something good and pleasing. Yet in truth, it can be more deadly for us than we even know.

Ultimate Lifesaver

The penalty for sinning against God was death. In fact, when God commanded Adam not to eat from the forbidden tree, he told Adam that he would surely die if he ever ate the fruit from the tree of the knowledge of good and evil. By choosing sin and eating from the forbidden tree, Adam and Eve brought on the penalty of death not only for themselves, but for all of humanity for thousands of years to come.

Despite their rebellion from his command and bringing about the consequences of their sin, we see God restoring a relationship with Adam and Eve.[17] We see from the beginning of time, God has always had a plan to restore our relationship with him.

God's desire for a relationship with us has outweighed our rebellion against him.

His plan for our salvation was not an afterthought. In fact, scripture tells us that Jesus was slain from the creation of the earth.[18] That does not mean he actually died before the earth was created, but it does mean that God in his foreknowledge knew that we would rebel from him and had already planned ahead for it. He understood humanity would need a way to restore and reconcile our relationship with him.

The truth is that his desire to be with us outweighs our inadequacy to be with him. We have all fallen short of the glory of God, not some, not most... all.[19] It is when we realize we cannot meet the level of God's goodness without Christ that we see the necessity of Christ's death and resurrection.

Despite our sin and our rebellion, God still sent his son to die to pay for the sins of humanity. God gave everything that he had to have a relationship with us.

Our sin is not something that should be quickly read through, passed by, or given a mere nod. We must take the knowledge of our sin against the God of the universe seriously and think through the implications of our actions. If we undervalue or misunderstand the true sacrifice of Jesus on the cross, we can end up feeling indifferent towards sin in our life. If we don't fully understand Jesus' death and resurrection, then we may begin to rationalize our sin. Over time, this is how a lifestyle of sin becomes the 'new norm' in our lives.

To come into a relationship with God and to remove the penalty for our sin, we must merely repent. What does repentance look like? Repentance is a change of mind, an awareness and confession of sin, and an acceptance of God as our Savior and Lord.

When we walk in repentance, we alter the lens through which we live. Repentance acknowledges that God's way is better than ours. Repentance also means that we turn away from the place we were in, and head in a new and different direction. We choose to walk towards the life that God has designed us to live.

Performance-Based Christianity

Once we put our trust in the work of Christ, we can step out of the curse of sin and into a reconciled relationship with God. However, upon receiving salvation through faith, there frequently seems to be a gravitational pull towards performance-based Christianity.

Performance-based Christianity is when we put our trust in our works and not in Christ's work through faith. A performance-based lifestyle is one marked on the outside by a life of good works, and one characterized within by a false belief that the number of good works will determine our outcome on the other side of eternity. This belief comes from a misunderstanding of the Gospel and a misconstrued concept of grace.

Performance-based Christianity is what I like to call Gold Star Christianity.

If you grew up in a church like mine, we were continually getting gold stars in our Sunday school classes. We received them for Bible reading, church attendance, verse memorizations, and other acts of accomplishment. Gold stars were not necessarily a bad thing. However, they served to form a relationship with God that was shaped more by recognition for my work, than for the work of Christ. Unfortunately, for some people as they mature and lead their Christian lives, their lives are still marked more by what they do rather than by their intimacy with God.

Jesus tells us that only through him may we enter eternal life. Through his death and resurrection, we have been offered a gift, the gift of eternal life. We must be willing to accept that it is not by our merit, nor by our performance, or by our own will, that we are given the opportunity to enter eternity.

Sometimes, this performance-based mindset comes from our misunderstanding of the true meaning of grace. Without fully understanding God's grace, we can be led to believe that we can actually be saved through our good works.

> *"For it is by grace you have been saved,*
> *through faith – and this is not from*
> *yourselves, it is the gift of God – not by*
> *works so that no one can boast."[20]*

Grace is often defined as the unmerited favor of God. Unmerited. Unearned. Undeserved. Unjustified. Am I getting my point across?

It was because of grace that we can be saved. There is nothing we can do to earn it because he loved us before we ever knew him. Even when we are at our worst, God loves us. Do not all of a sudden believe that you must earn his love, for that is religion at its worst.

The truth of grace is that when we are not "performing" at

our best, God's love is still pouring over us. Our value is not caught up in our performance. Accepting this truth will lead us toward the freedom in his love that God intended for us.

We cannot influence the love God has for our lives with our good works. When we understand that we cannot change God, this dissipates any pressure to perform. And when addressed this way, we see the ridiculousness of the thought.

We can, however, grow in our understanding of his love for us. Note that this is not a change in God's love, it is merely a change in our perspective.

Have you ever known someone who could not trust others to do anything? It may have been your parents, your boss, or a friend, or it may have even been yourself. Yet trusting in ourselves isn't actually trust, but a messed-up version of control. People fail to trust for many reasons: because they have a fear of failure, because they want to control events and people around them, or because they have suffered pain from doing so before and cannot bring themselves to trust again.

Our performance often comes from an inward attempt or desire to be our own personal savior, something we simply cannot be. Why does it seem more comfortable to put trust in our own works rather than in the cross of Christ?

I believe one of the main reasons is that we don't want to be helpless and we don't want to be perceived as weak. So, to avoid those personal pitfalls, we create a world in which we believe we can save ourselves by our own good works. Our performance, however, is still rebellion against God. It is an attempt to put our trust in something other than what we should: in Jesus and in his sacrifice for us upon the cross.

Looking back in history to the time of the disciples, we

see instances when they nearly fell into such a performance-based trap. In Luke 10, we see Jesus sending his disciples out to the surrounding towns to preach about the kingdom of God. They returned with much excitement and began to tell Jesus what happened on their journeys.

Who could blame them after seeing God move in miraculous ways on their missionary journey?

However, we then see Jesus not curbing their excitement, but ensuring that their priorities were in order.

> *"However, do not rejoice that the spirits*
> *submit to you, but rejoice that your names*
> *are written in heaven."[21]*

We were not intended to get caught up in what we are doing, but revel in the fact that we are known by God while doing it. If we forget that we are known by him, then we may fall into doing works to try to earn the right to be loved.

Rules and Regulations

Christianity is also not about legalistically following a set of rules and regulations, even though this is a common misconception many people have. God did not create the commandments with the intent to control us. He created the commandments to have a relationship with his people. For us, the end result of following God's law is not a pat on the back or a gold star sticker for our effort. No, the end result of following God's design for our lives is for us to walk in deeper intimacy with him.

The Apostle Paul was a champion for grace in the first-century church. Grace not only saves us from our performance-based mindset, but also allows us to loosen our grip on our belief that following a set of rules will save us. In many of Paul's letters to the churches, we see him championing grace. In his letter to the Galatians he writes:

> *"I am astonished that you are so quickly*
> *deserting the one who called you to live in*
> *the grace of Christ and are turning to a*
> *different gospel - which is really no gospel*
> *at all. Evidently some people are throwing*
> *you into confusion and are trying to*
> *pervert the gospel of Christ."[22]*

At this point in time, some teachers said the Gentile believers had to follow the laws and customs of the Jewish culture to be saved. Yet, this goes against the true message of the gospel. Salvation is not the result of following the law, but it is through the death and resurrection of Jesus in which we are saved.

Paul continued his argument in the following passages, stating that grace is what is at the center of the true gospel, not the law.

> *"I do not set aside the grace of God, for if*
> *righteousness could be gained through the*
> *law, Christ died for nothing."[23]*

Paul was opposing those who said they believed in Christ but were still commanding people to follow the law, saying it would make them more acceptable to God. Paul is not denying the role of the law as a vital part of our relationship with God; he was merely stating that the law will not prove our worth to a God of grace.

We also see Jesus coming face-to-face with people who

were commanding others to do more than what was commanded in scripture without doing it themselves. The Pharisees, religious leaders in Jesus' time, had created a wall around God's law to keep people from sinning against God. They built this "wall" by creating more rules for people to follow. These rules were not designed and commanded by God but rather by mere humans.

Jesus did not tell the Pharisees that what they were trying to accomplish was necessarily wrong. However, he said it was their hypocrisy that was wrong because they were doing them not to bring glory to God, but rather to be noticed by other people. Jesus told them, their heart was in the wrong place. Has there been a time where your heart in this area has been in the wrong place as well?

This can be a significant performance-based trap for our life with Christ. We want to be noticed for what we are doing rather than doing it because it is what God has called us to do. While what we are doing can be good, if our heart's motive is in the wrong place then we may be doing the right thing for the wrong reasons. And while things may look good and merit praise from others, God will not be satisfied with mere actions.

He wants our heart.

He wants us.

Setting ourselves free of this performance minded relationship with God is something that can be extremely difficult. It may take years of work and prayer to walk into the freedom that Christ has given us in his grace, but being released from this performance-based lifestyle has its glorious rewards. It merely comes through repentance and the renewing of our mind.

God is willing to teach you how not to base your relationship on your performance. In fact, by opening your heart to the relationship he has designed for you, you will begin to understand that his love was never, and will never, be shaped by any such performance or good deeds here on Earth.

THE HOLY SPIRIT'S ROLE

Have you ever been introduced to someone you don't know? You may have heard about this person from a friend, but without a prior meeting, that person is only a name, merely a description.

For some, this chapter will make them feel as if they are being introduced to someone they do not know. For others, this chapter will be repetitive, and you may even question why this chapter is included in the book.

Human nature leads us to ignore what we don't understand. This may happen to the Holy Spirit and his role in our lives because he has been misunderstood by us. Ultimately, we need to allow scripture to define who the Holy Spirit is, and what the Holy Spirit's role in our lives will be. We need to do this because the Holy Spirit is essential to our relationship with God.

There have been many people who have overlooked the Holy Spirit because he has been presented as something unexplainable, even weird, out-of-date, spooky, or a ghost-like-something talked about in the back room of a church. In some people's minds, they do not desire to have the Holy

Spirit living inside of them because of the uncertain ways in which others have portrayed him.

The Holy Spirit is an integral part of what we call the Trinity: God, Jesus, and the Holy Spirit. As the third part of the Trinity, he does everything with the intent of leading us into a greater knowledge of who God truly is.

In John 16, we see Jesus telling the disciples about the Holy Spirit who is going to come when he leaves Earth. He even tells his disciples that it is better if he leaves and the Holy Spirit comes.[24] I imagine them thinking there was no way that this statement could have be true. How could it be better if Jesus was gone? They didn't even understand how the Holy Spirit would look and how living with the Holy Spirit would feel. Despite their uncertainty Jesus was advising them to value the Holy Spirit's role in their lives.

Do we treat Jesus' words as truth today?

We need to make sure that we understand and appreciate the Holy Spirit's role in our lives. We can no longer underestimate and overlook his purpose in our walk with God.

If we believe we can fulfill God's desire and design for a relationship outside of the work of the Holy Spirit, then we are misguided. The Holy Spirit enables us to understand God's design for our relationship and to which direction we should head. God gives us a sequence of stages through the Holy Spirit that we are to follow.

We will only be able to follow, if we are led by the Holy Spirit. We will be unable to accomplish the walk God desires and has designed for us, outside of the Holy Spirit's work in our lives. Simply put, we cannot do this alone. God gave us the Holy Spirit, to enable us to walk the desired path of our destiny! Without the Holy Spirit guiding us, we are as good as trying to build furniture without any directions.

Unfortunately, this chapter will not be able to cover the

entirety of the Holy Spirit's role in our lives. It would take many books to do so. We will, however, look at some central and vital aspects of our relationship with the Holy Spirit. Before we begin to see the Holy Spirit's role in our lives, let's look at what it means to be filled by the Holy Spirit.

Be Filled

When we are filled with anything other than the Holy Spirit, we aren't able to walk in God's specific design for an intimate relationship with him. We were designed to be filled with the Holy Spirit and walk under his influence. What would you think if you ordered a drink at Starbucks and when you brought it up to your lips instead of the sweet taste of coffee, you drank runny mashed potatoes? Silly yes, but coffee cups are designed to hold coffee, just as we are intended to be filled with the Holy Spirit.

> *"Don't be drunk with wine, because that will ruin your life. Instead, be filled with the Holy Spirit."*[25]

Paul contrasts being filled with the Holy Spirit with that of being drunk with wine. What he is essentially saying is that we should be under the control of the Holy Spirit, not the influence of alcohol or any other outside source. Paul urges us to be under the influence of the Holy Spirit, following his leading and obeying what he asks us to do.

As we walk with the Holy Spirit, our capacity to grow in our relationship with him increases. He can fill us up more because we have expanded our capacity to be filled by knowing him more. When we are not filled with the Holy

Spirit, we are not fully capable of accomplishing his true design for our lives.

To fully understand the role of the Holy Spirit in our relationship with God, we must first be filled by him.

We cannot be filled by the Holy Spirit while quenching him at the same time. When we do this, we miss out on the beautiful blessing that comes with being led by the Holy Spirit. Quenching the Spirit is similar to when you put out a fire with a large bucket of water. The passion, love, and adoration that we have for our relationship with God can be nearly extinguished when we turn away from the work of the Holy Spirit.

We are commanded by God's Word not to quench the Holy Spirit.[26] But what does this mean? For many years of my life, I was unaware of this command. I didn't know what it truly meant, nor did I realize that I was doing just that: quenching the Holy Spirit's ability to lead and direct me. To better walk in faith with the Holy Spirit, we need to understand the implications and what it looks like to quench him.

How exactly does quenching the Holy Spirit show up in our lives? How do we know that we are quenching him? There are a few specific instances where we can see that we are extinguishing the work of the Holy Spirit. They include difficulty hearing his voice, and not walking in the gifts of the Holy Spirit. It also includes falling out of the passion for our walk with God and prayer.

When we quench the spirit, it sometimes leads us to difficulty in hearing God speak to us. Most often for me, God's voice comes through reading his Word. However, there are times where he speaks through small, quiet impressions. When we quench the Spirit, not only do we not desire to dig into his Word, we also overwhelm those quiet impressions and become painfully unaware of their presence in our lives.

We cannot fulfill God's desire and purpose for our relationship with him when we aren't living with and opening up to the work of the Holy Spirit. When we do this to the Holy Spirit, we may find ourselves walking down the wrong path, heading in the wrong directions, and making mistakes we wish we hadn't. Only when we are filled with the Spirit and led by his promptings are we able to walk in his plan for our lives. Walking in the Spirit will also give us a more profound sense of fulfillment that only he can provide us with.

Another way we can see that we are quenching the Holy Spirit is when we are not walking in the gifts and fruits of the Holy Spirit.

We discover this through the life of Timothy, who was a young pastor in the New Testament. We see that he was encouraged in scripture not to neglect his spiritual gifts.[27] We need to receive this and walk in our spiritual gifts as he did. When we fail to walk in the spiritual gifts God has given us, we also disregarding the Holy Spirit's role in our lives. He is the one who empowers us to walk into the fullness of these spiritual gifts, and when we are not walking in them we are essentially telling him that we don't really need him.

We can also tell if we are quenching him if we aren't seeing the fruit of the Holy Spirit revealed in our lives. The fruit of the Holy Spirit is not a target of behaviors that we should aim for, but a litmus test for us to see if we are being led by the Holy Spirit. We don't try to walk in joy to be filled with the Holy Spirit, but rather when we are filled with him we will walk in joy because of his presence in our lives. The fruit of the Spirit is love, joy, peace, forbearance, kindness, goodness, faithfulness, gentleness, and self-control.[28]

Do a self-check of those things in your life: Are you living a loving, joyful, peaceful life? If we are guilty of pushing away the work of the Holy Spirit, we will often struggle walking in peace, love, goodness, or any of the other fruit.

Another symptom of quenching the Holy Spirit is not walking in passion. Similar to putting the fire out with water, when we quench him we also douse our passion for following God.

Maybe you started off as a passionate Christian and some-where along the way you lost it. You are not sure where it went or how you lost it, but you know that you are missing the passion you once had/felt with God. I believe that in some way, this may be because you are quenching the Spirit.

We may also be guilty of quenching the Holy Spirit if our heart for prayer is burnt out. The Holy Spirit is crazy about prayer. In fact, God's Word says that he is praying for us, even when we aren't praying for ourselves. We are to pray in the Spirit in all occasions.[29] We frequently treat prayer in such a ritualistic way, but the Holy Spirit will teach us what to pray and when to pray for it. He will serve as a guide for not only our lives, for but our prayer life as well, as we learn how to better follow him.

The solution to these difficulties isn't trying harder or putting in more hours. Many times, when it comes to finding a solution, we try to accomplish it through our own strength. However, it is not by our own strength that we will see the answer to the difficulties we face, but it is through the power of the Holy Spirit. The solution is found through submitting to the work of the Holy Spirit and being filled by him.

Too Busy

I love multitasking and keeping myself busy. I tend to think that I am quite good at doing many things at once and accomplishing more. However, the times that I'm multitasking are also times that I end up quenching the Spirit's work in my life even more.

In this very moment, I am writing on my iPad with two computers open on my desk. Where does the Holy Spirit fit into my small office that's filled with technology? I'm not exactly sure.

This doesn't mean that technology or any other worldly distraction is necessarily the work of the devil. Just as with anything, technology is great, but it's how we use it and prioritize it that determines how much room we have remaining to designate to the Holy Spirit.

Succumbing to busyness may be one of the primary ways in which we quench the Holy Spirit. We live in a current culture that idolizes busyness. If we all had a dollar for every time we asked someone how they were doing, and their answer was busy, we would all be very rich.

In turn, we tend to project this expectation and look down upon people who are not busy or doing enough with their lives. Perhaps we believe that if we aren't busy trying to accomplish something, then our value to society will be in question.

Can we not be busy, perhaps even be still, and be a productive member of society?

Ask yourself: when was the last time you slowed down long enough to spend time with God? When did you last hear that still, quiet voice and walk in obedience to the Holy Spirits promptings? Do you feel like your busyness is getting in the way of your relationship with God?

These questions aren't being asked to condemn you in any way. Neither are they meant to judge. Hopefully, asking these thoughtful but straightforward questions will help you to stop and discern where you are in your walk with God, and decide whether or not your busyness is quenching the Spirit's work in your life.

This time of reflection doesn't always require massive amounts of time on your part. Know that the Holy Spirit will show up in every place you let him. Your place of work, your house, while your washing dishes, doing laundry, changing a diaper.

Even while writing a book.

Now let's look at what scripture says about the role of the Holy Spirit as he guides and comforts us.

Guide

The Holy Spirit will guide you into all truth.[30] The truth about what? He will lead us into the truth about Christ and the truth about the life we are to live. The truth about everything needed for us to walk the journey that God has planned for us.

The ultimate goal of his guidance into truth is that it leads us to freedom. We are all, every one of us, in trouble without the work of the Holy Spirit's leading. Many people throughout the world are not walking in freedom. But recognize the power of the Holy Spirit can lead us out of the slavery of sin and into the freedom that Christ bought for us on the cross.

One of the hardest concepts as a believer is to not fall back into the slavery we were bound to before we experienced the power of the cross. The work of the Holy Spirit will always lead us away from our bondage and into the destiny he has designed for us to live.

Many have likened the Holy Spirit to be a sort of spiritual GPS. While this is well-meaning, and I do believe he does give us steps in the next direction, the analogy misses many aspects of the Holy Spirit's true capacity. The Holy Spirit cannot be lowered to some computer-generated voice that merely tells us what turns to make. When we call the Holy Spirit a GPS, we effectively remove his personality from the picture, limiting the role of the Holy Spirit's role in our lives.

MapQuest was one of the original online sites, before GPS in our cell phones, for people to type in a destination, and receive a printout with step-by-step directions. You would take the paper with you that mapped out the entire route and read each step along the way. Modern-day GPS with directions being orally provided makes the days of using MapQuest seem antiquated, yet at the time it was the easiest and most helpful way to travel.

People often times desire this exact 'solution' to the destiny of their lives, in a relationship with God. We want to see the entire plan, well mapped-out and easy to understand. We want to know not only the destination but all the steps along the way before we even want to set off on the journey.

The Holy Spirit is not like MapQuest; he doesn't provide us with the entire journey in one, quick download. He will typically tell us where we are going in step-by-step directions one at a time. Essentially, providing us with the steps that we can handle until the next.

This careful, step-by-step planning allows him the opportunity to show us his trustworthiness. If we did have all the directions, we would have no need to trust, rely, or depend on the Holy Spirit at all. We may even be tempted to skip steps and make the route we are headed much shorter than God has designed it to be. If we had all our life steps, we could very well lose sight of the fact that we need God and the Holy Spirit's guiding direction in our lives.

God wants to be with us every step of our lives, as it is designed to be.

The Holy Spirit's role as a guide is similar to that of a Sherpa. The Sherpa are a group of people who guide people intending to climb Mount Everest in Nepal. Sherpa's have been guiding people up the sides of Mount Everest since the beginning of mountain climbing started.

Sherpas are in charge of helping people not only climb the mountain by guiding them up the challenging terrain, but they also do much of the work to get them all to the top of the mountain. Fully acclimated to the changes in temperature, oxygen levels, and conditions, they carry oxygen tanks up and down the mountain so people can continue to breathe comfortably at heights lacking oxygen. They also carry the most weight of anyone on these journeys. They serve as guides, helpers, and mentors along the route.

There have been a few people who've climbed Mount Everest without the guidance of one of these local Sherpas. To some, it may be crazy to think about attempting this endeavor on their own and leaving behind the people who know the most about Mount Everest. Unfortunately, this place is where many Christians are in their walk with God. They try to walk in an intimate relationship with God, outside of the Holy Spirit's guidance. We may try to do this because we are unaware of the Holy Spirit's role in our lives. Or maybe because we've become impatient with our progress, or because we've developed a lack of trust in God.

Though it's been proven possible to climb Everest alone, it is impossible to walk in an intimate relationship with God without our own guiding Sherpa, the Holy Spirit. The Holy

Spirit is the most trustworthy guide we could ever hope to have.

The Holy Spirit should be viewed as our ever-present guide. He never leaves us, nor does he forsake us. Ever.

Imagine if you were climbing Mount Everest and your Sherpa guide suddenly decided to turn around and leave you where you stood? Hopefully, Sherpas wouldn't ever do such a thing, but the Holy Spirit will never walk away from us. Instead, he walks with us and leads us into the destiny that God has designed for our lives.

He is indeed the best guide that we could ever ask for!

Comparing the Holy Spirit to a Sherpa, although valuable, still falls somewhat short of who he is. Such analogies provide insight into who he wants us to be in a relationship, yet unlike a Sherpa guide who stays with a climber for his ascent and descent and then leaves, the Holy Spirit is with us forever.

He is our guide for eternity, not merely for a momentary adventure.

Comforter

The Holy Spirit also serves as our comforter.[31] He always comes alongside us in our current circumstances and provides the comfort we need to walk in the situation we are in. Of course, implied in this understanding is the scary truth that we need a comforter.

There will be times when we absolutely need to have someone there to get us through circumstances. This is a job for which the Holy Spirit is well-equipped. He is always there for us despite the situation we face, he is willing to lead us into peace. Our comforter gives us peace that passes all understanding.[32]

Have you ever met someone who, despite obviously difficult circumstances, was at peace with what was going on around them?

I once heard a story about two brothers who'd enlisted to fight in World War 2 and were assigned to the same regiment. One night, after they had moved through a fierce battle, they were issued a command to dig foxholes for themselves. Foxholes were holes dug in the ground so soldiers could try to protect themselves from incoming artillery and sniper fire.

Even though they had just been in one of the fiercest battles that they had yet to see, the men began to dig their holes. All through the night, they dug. The holes needed to be deep enough for them to fit in so that they could escape the oncoming attack. One brother was so tired from the previous battle that instead of continuing to dig out his foxhole, he accidentally fell asleep. Through the night, as the other soldiers dug, this brother remained sound asleep.

As soon as the sun rose the next morning, the expected battle began, and bullets started to fly. From the cover of his foxhole, the brother who spent all night digging noticed his brother yards away, lying flat on the ground. He immediately believed the worst and thought his brother to be dead. When the bullets ceased, he climbed out of his foxhole and ran over to his brother's prone body.

Yet to his extreme disbelief, he found his brother alive. He was still asleep. When he fell asleep from his exhaustion the night before, he never woke up even during the crazy conditions surrounding him.

This is how the Holy Spirit works in our lives, in our own circumstances. While we may face the most difficult battle we have ever seen, if we are led by the Holy Spirit we can calmly walk through it.

The world could blow up all around us, and still, we can

be as calm as if nothing was happening. We don't ignore our circumstances, nor do we avoid them or pretend they don't exist. We simply walk in peace, joy, and patience as the Holy Spirit comforts us. When we open ourselves to allow the Holy Spirit to provide comfort, we can be seemingly stuck in the middle of life's toughest battles and always find peace.

5

RELATIONSHIPGOALS

The second part of this book takes a look at some of God's relationship goals. Unfortunately, we won't be able to cover all of the relationship goals God wants to have with us. That would require a much larger book or a series of books that would go on forever. However, we will cover a few primary relationship goals that include friendship, fatherhood, marriage, promises and others.

The goal of this book is to ignite your appetite for God's desire for your relationship with him, not to provide an entire list of relationship goals. This book also won't give you a comprehensive report on every relationship goal. It was written to provide a glimpse of the invitations for different relationship goals that God has for our life with him.

As you read the following chapters, you will see into a window of what I have learned as I walked with God in these different relationship goals.

Each chapter will cover specific aspects of these relationship goal that God desires to have with us. As you read through the chapters, you may wonder if and why I have failed to address an aspect of a particular relationship goal.

You may ask: Why did he leave that out of the friendship relationship goal? Or how did he miss several parts when it comes to the marriage relationship goal? I want to encourage you to write down those aspects that you see missing from a certain relationship goal.

As you begin to write them down, ask yourself, why is this aspect important to me? Why is this important to God? Have I fully developed this part of my relationship with God? If not what is missing?

I also want to encourage you to work through the book in its entirety. Read through each relationship goal before you start to write out your first relationship goal with God. This is because as you read, you may feel as if you want to begin the relationship goal with God that you just read about. However, you may miss out on the relationship goal that God wants you to start if you don't first read through the entire book.

Also, as you read you may encounter aspects of your own Christian walk that aren't yet fully developed. This shouldn't make you feel as if you are any less of a Christian. Indeed, this is not how God works, nor is it my intention in writing this book. God isn't condemning you because he knows that we are not fully developed.

Most often, when we become aware of a shortcoming in a particular area, it is because the Holy Spirit is telling us that this will be the area of the next miracle in our lives. It is most often a virtual indicator that shows us where he is going to work in our lives!

We also can't walk in condemnation when God begins to show us his relationship goal for our life. When he does show us our relationship goal, it is a picture of his desire for our relationship. When God shares his desire with us, it is a preferred picture of what our future relationship can and will look like!

However, when we are confronted with his desire, it may look different than the relationship that we have with him at this point in time. This doesn't mean that we won't ever get there, but it does mean that our relationship with him will undoubtedly change.

My hope for you is that by the end of the book, you would begin living in and writing about your own, unique relationship goal with God.

So, let's begin with the first relationship goal in this book: Friendship.

6

FRIENDSHIP

John 15:12-15 NIV
My command is this: Love each other as I have loved
you. Greater love has no one than this: to lay down
one's life for one's friends. You are my friends if you
do what I command. I no longer call you servants
because a servant does not know my master's
business. Instead, I have called you friends, for
everything that I learned from the Father I have made
known to you.

True Friend

Have you ever met someone who has a friendship with God?
You would know if you have because of the way they talk
about him and walk with him. If someone had asked me when
I began writing this chapter if I had a friendship with Jesus,
my answer would have been - absolutely!

I knew Jesus was my friend and I would have proved it to
you by reading John 15.

However, when I came in contact with the first person

who had an authentic friendship with Jesus, I realized that my friendship was only on paper. It wasn't a real, genuine functioning friendship. My friendship looked more like one from social media rather than a true authentic friendship.

This man whom I met was 'real' when he opened his mouth about Jesus. I could tell that he actually knew him, that they were friends. It was as if they spent every day with each other, talking as friends will do. I am guessing that they may even do fun things together, staying up late together and enjoying each other's company.

When this man told others about Jesus, he opened the conversation with the simple fact that Jesus was his best friend.

It was at this point that I realized I didn't have a real friendship with Jesus, at least not a functioning one. In my mind, I knew that Jesus wanted to be my friend, but I had no clue what that friendship should look like, day-to-day.

So, that was the day that I told Jesus I wanted to be his friend. Not because I knew it was the right thing to do, but because I desired to experience an authentic friendship with him.

Jesus is inviting you into a friendship with him. Not one where you talk about him because of what you have read but because you have spent time with him. Gotten to know him. Loved him.

Intimate Friendships

A friend once revealed to me that he felt as if he did not have any truly intimate friendships. I completely understood where he was coming from because there have been many times when I have felt the same.

I listened, allowing him to share his feelings and angst,

and then asked him what he thought a close friendship should look like. He then told me that he really didn't know.

I would guess that many people have no idea what true friendship looks like. We may not know because we have never had a close friendship on this Earth. We may have had what we thought was a close relationship or one that moved in and out of closeness through the years. But was it ever what we desired in a friendship?

I have never, honestly had a best friend. Or at least never felt as if I did. In fact, I can remember throughout my high school years that I desperately wanted to have one. Typical of that age, I wanted to be best friends with the coolest people in the room. Yet I always felt rejected by them.

Many days, I felt as if no one in the world wanted to be my friend. Perhaps you've experienced it, too. Or maybe you were always the coolest person in the room, and some people only wanted to be your friend because of your popularity. Yet while being the most popular kid, maybe you still lacked close friendships because no one around you genuinely valued you for who you were.

Without knowing what your story of friendships are, I do know that Jesus has invited us into a relationship that many of us on this earth have failed to achieve with those around us.

I wonder if we have lost the definition of true friendship because of the introduction of social media into our world. We 'add friend' and 'like,' we 'follow' and 'share,' too many of us believing that we can have friendships with hundreds if not thousands of people simply because we're connected online. We maintain these 'friendships' by liking and commenting on their posts. We are sometimes 'friends' with people who we never see face-to-face, we may never have human contact with these people.

Can we really know someone by merely looking at their status and the pictures they post?

We cannot, of course, push all the blame on technology and social media for our lack of real friendships. In some ways, social media has allowed us to stay connected more than ever before. However, some could rightfully argue that it has taken away from the deep connection we're able to have with one another.

Because of the virtual world in which we live, I think in many ways it affects how we treat Jesus' invitation for friendship. We treat him like an Instagram hero and look at his life in awe. Then we miss out on the intimate relationship that he has designed for us to have through a friendship with him.

We cannot honestly know someone merely through a computer or a phone screen in the same way we can't know God if we keep him at a distance. If we haven't had great friendships in the world, we may end up settling. Settling for a virtual friendship with others and with Jesus, rather than a real one.

Jesus says that he chose us.[33] He doesn't want us on the other side of a phone screen. He invites us in closer for a real and authentic friendship.

Jesus doesn't merely add us to a list of his friends and like our posts. He doesn't follow us on Twitter or Instagram. A friendship with Jesus is much more profound than anything we can find online.

He will begin to teach us how to walk in friendship with him. The best part is we are always offered an invitation to be friends.

Are you friends with Jesus? Do you spend time with him? Do you ask him questions like great friends would? Like how was his day? How is he feeling? We need to stop behaving as if all we can do is like and comment on his statuses.

Jesus is alive and living, and he is calling us into an intimate friendship.

What is holding you back from connecting with Jesus as a friend? For me, it was a deeply held belief that I was not good enough. When we don't believe Jesus likes us or wants to be our friend, it's likely because we don't like ourselves. You might even think that you wouldn't be your own friend.

Jesus broke through all of my insecurities when I realized that he wanted to be my friend. He desired to be my friend. He wants a friendship with you too. No matter how unable you may consider yourself to be friends with Jesus, he chose you as his friend.

My desire to have a best friend was never satisfied until I began a friendship with Jesus. Your desire to have a friend will also never be adequately fulfilled until you walk with God as his friend.

Servant or Friend?

Jesus says in John 15 that he no longer calls us servants but rather friends. So, which one are we supposed to be? A servant of God, or a friend? What if, in God's view, these roles weren't so different? What if best friends behaved as a servant? What if servants ended up making the best of friends?

I believe that as we learn how to be servants of Christ, we can also grow into a deepening friendship with him. Jesus says there is no greater love than to lay one's life down for friends.[34] This is an excellent definition of service; we have to die to our own desires and sacrifice for others to develop genuine friendships. Best friends know how to serve one another.

This journey into a friendship with Jesus is often a long

journey. Not because God makes it that way, but because we make this more difficult than it should be. Sometimes, we would rather be a servant than we would be a friend of God. Being a servant of God may be more 'comfortable' because we end up treating God as a controlling master. All we have to do is obey what he tells us. To this end, we turn our slavery into our religion, liking the structure of rule following.

Friendship, on the other hand, is more difficult; it isn't defined by keeping rules. It is first and utmost about the relationship.

Jesus said if you are my friends then you will obey what I command. When our heart is set on a friendship with Jesus, then we desire to obey what he has commanded. We do so because we understand that his design for life is what's best. We maintain a relationship with him not because he is a strict friend who bosses us around, but because we understand that a real friendship happens within the commands of Jesus.

We see this desire to follow God's commands through the life of Abraham. Abraham's relationship with God was described as a friendship in several places throughout scripture because of his deep, thriving relationship with God.[35] He gives us a great example of how God's friends have a willingness to follow his commandments.

Abraham didn't follow God's commands because he wanted a relationship with God. Instead, he followed them because he knew God and trusted him. Obedience does not develop a friendship with Jesus. It is our friendship with him that develops a heart of obedience.

When we realize that Jesus is our friend, his commands become a delight rather than a duty. We aren't merely serving him because we are obligated. Instead, we delight in serving Jesus as our friend.

Great and real friends will do anything for one another.

Jesus modeled this commitment by going to the cross for our friendship. He died to be not only our savior but also our friend.

We see the beauty of God's relationship goals in this conversation about being a servant or friend, as well. We don't stop becoming a servant of Christ because he has called us a friend. Just like we don't stop being the bride of Christ because God is our father. God's relationship goals are inter-woven. We don't lose one relationship with him because he is teaching us another. And in most instances, what we have learned in one relationship goal transitions and helps us learn through other relationship goals, as well.

A Great Friend

Besides Jesus, my wife, Talia, has been the best friend I have ever had. She is the best representation as to what a great friendship should and could look like. She is fantastic at making friends and going out of her way to develop and maintain friendships with people she interacts with.

While Talia would tell you that she is far from perfect and still learning how to maintain friendships, she is better than anyone I know at being an excellent friend. One of the most vital aspects to my wife's ability to develop real friendships is her unique ability to listen.

Talia lets friends know they are heard. Whenever she sits down with people, they feel a significant amount of love because of her ability to listen. Many people want to be around her because of the love that she has for those around her.

Maybe you don't have a friend who is willing to listen to you the way that you have desired. Jesus is our friend and is willing to listen to you, even into the middle of the night about what you are going through. He wants you to share your heart with him. Whatever you are going through, he will hear you out.

This may be a foreign concept to you, but I want you right now to tell Jesus what you are going through. It doesn't have to be complicated or sad. He wants to hear the good things, too Jesus is our friend and wants to hear about everything we are going through. Talking to him about what is going on in our lives will help us further develop our friendship with him.

Not only does Talia listen well, she also goes out of her way to support her friends. A few years ago, she had a friend whose father had passed away. While she didn't know this person extremely well at the time, she felt compelled to attend the man's funeral. Talia even rescheduled her own vacation to go to the funeral. I could never have guessed how much this action would mean to this friend, but it was the beginning of a deep and meaningful friendship they now have.

This story reminds me of a passage we find in scripture when Jesus returned to his friends who were mourning the loss of a loved one.

In John 11:17-37, we see Jesus raising Lazarus from the dead. Before he performed any such miracle, though, he wept with Mary and Martha. Jesus wept with them in the worst moment of their life. We see the humanity of Jesus at that moment, as he mourned with friends who were mourning.

Jesus will be with us in our worst moments.

He is the friend we can count on who will always be there.

Jesus will comfort us in moments when we don't think we can continue. He will lead us when we don't see any way out. He will be the friend that we need no matter the situation that we are in.

Jesus may not raise any of our family members from the dead, but he does want to resurrect a friendship with each of us if we don't yet have one with him.

Picked Up Right Where We Left Off

Have you ever had the kind of friend, where even if you haven't recently spent time together, you're able to pick up right where you left off?

I had a friend whom I hadn't seen or talked to in three years. We talked on the phone once or twice, but we hadn't spent any time together. He moved to Australia to serve as a youth pastor soon after we'd met. Fortunately for me, I was already set to travel to Australia for a few weeks to do some missions work. When we saw each other, we picked up right where we'd left off as soon as he met me at the airport. It seemed as if the last three years apart had never happened.

Despite this friend whom I was able to reconnect with, I have many friends I've met and yet haven't been able to reconnect with them. It seems as if time and space can really get in between friendships like this and it leads to a distancing in our relationships.

Have you ever felt as if in your relationship with Christ is the same? Maybe you've walked away from Jesus' invitation to friendship, and it's been years since you've walked in relationship with him.

Maybe you have felt like God is looking down upon you in disgust because you walked away from a relationship. Perhaps you see him as a judgmental friend because you weren't always there for him. This fallacy could not be farther from the truth! God is the farthest thing from that so-called, some-of-the time friend.

Unfortunately, I believe that this is how many of us view

our friendship with God. While we may talk to him once in a while, we never honestly get to connect with him. Maybe he visits us for a short time, and we get to spend time together, but then it all fades away.

This is not what Jesus intended for our friendship with him. He isn't far away. He is right next to you, and he wants to offer you an everyday friendship that will last for eternity!

If you have walked away from Jesus' invitation to a relationship, I believe that he wants to pick up right where you left off.

At the beginning of picking up where we left off, it may seem as if God doesn't want to talk much about the past. This is because his primary concern is in reconnecting with you, not reminiscing about what happened in the past. Jesus doesn't shame us when we return to him. There is no condemnation in Christ, and he is more concerned about our restoration than he is about pointing out our mistakes.

If you have fallen away from your relationship with Jesus, are you ready to pick up with him where you left off?

Invitation

God has been inviting people into a friendship with him for a long time. Both Abraham and Moses had deep and long-lasting friendships with God.

Moses was often referred to as God's friend. We see that the Lord would speak to Moses just as one speaks to a friend.[36] We also see Moses asking God to know him more. This almost always happens in friendships. We will want to know more about each other, and when we begin to know God as our friend, we will continually want to learn more about him.

Moses developed a deep friendship with God as he led the

nation of Israel out of slavery. We see him repeatedly going up the mountain, or going into the tent of meeting, and making time for God. Moses developed a sincere desire to be with God. From the burning bush in Exodus 3 we see his desire to know and be in an intimate relationship grow.

For years, I believed that Israel was never invited into God's presence like Moses was. I questioned why Moses was the only person in the nation referred to as God's friend. The truth is they were all invited into God's presence.

In Exodus 20, the entire nation of Israel was on the edge of the mountain where God was present. It says the whole nation was trembling with fear and remained at a distance. They didn't want to go into God's presence because they were afraid and even believed that they may be risking their lives.

But Moses encouraged them not to be afraid. He had already been in the presence of God and said just as he hadn't died, neither would they. Still, the people remained at a distance, despite seeing Moses walking into the smoke where God's presence lay. Their fear got the better of them, and they weren't willing to say yes to the invitation that God had extended for their lives.

Through this, we see the entire nation of Israel missing out on an amazing opportunity to have an intimate relationship with God.

I am afraid too many people are living on the edge of a mountainous relationship with God but something holding them back. It may be fear. Or hurt. Or shame. Even disappointment.

Is there something keeping you from this type of friendship with God? What is it?

Remember that there is nothing that can separate us from the love of God. God will help remove anything that is keeping you from saying yes to his desire for your friendship with him.

When you do begin developing a friendship with Jesus, you will not want to miss a moment because you'll enjoy spending time with him. He is the best friend that you could have ever wished for. He wants to be your friend, not because he is obligated, but because he enjoys who you are.

Know that God has a place for you to develop a friendship with him. To do this, you may need to go to a place where you feel at peace and where you can be yourself.

For me, that place is out on the nearest lake or pond. I don't have a boat, but I enjoy standing on the shore, listening to the sounds of the water and fishing for hours at a time. I often imagine Jesus joining me on the shore and inviting me to be with him.

I have fished on those shores countless times with Jesus.

I have learned more about who God is from being alone with him.

I hope to encourage you to find your special place to spend time with God. Maybe it is at a lake, or on top of a mountain like Moses. Perhaps it is at a coffee shop, or at your home in a comfy chair. It honestly doesn't matter where this place is. What matters is that you find it, that you go there regularly, and that you spend quality time with God!

Remember, developing intimacy with God in whatever relationship goal takes time. Unlike expectations in our era, we cannot form a friendship with Jesus with just the click of a button.

7

FATHERHOOD

John 1:12-13 NIV
Yet to all who did receive him, to those who believed
in his name, he gave the right to become children of
God — children born not of natural descent, nor of
human decision or a husband's will, but born of God.

Show Us The Father

At one point in Jesus' ministry, he was asked by his disciples to show them the Father. His response was simple, "Anyone who has seen me has seen the Father."[37]

Jesus was a living, breathing, walking image of his father. His every move was an act of a son walking in a perfect relationship with the father. When we look at Jesus, we see what this Fatherhood relationship goal should ideally look like: a child walking in an intimate relationship with their father.

All of us have an inward desire to see the Father, our true father, and yet we live in a world that is often fatherless. Millions of children have grown up and to this day grow up without a father in their lives. Even if you grew up with your dad living in your household, he might have affected the way you view the Heavenly Father.

This is an attack that the enemy uses to keep us distant from a relationship with God. It makes sense that the enemy would try to attack one of the most intimate relationships we can have with God. He doesn't want us to be faithful sons and daughters. He is terrified of a world that is full of children of God. By preventing intimacy between a child and his or her father, he attacks our world and introduces widespread fatherlessness.

The enemy of our Heavenly Father will do anything possible to create a void in our earthly lives to ensure that we do not desire a relationship with our Heavenly Father. Satan doesn't want us to trust that God our father is good and trustworthy. He also doesn't want us to depend on him.

What our world needs are children who love, trust, and depend on their Heavenly Father.

Adopted

So how do we come into the family of God?

We are adopted into his family through the sacrifice of Jesus on the cross. When we by faith trust in Christ, we also receive the Holy Spirit who brings about the truth of our adoption.

In his letter to the Romans, Paul describes this process of adoption:

> *"For those who are led by the Spirit of God*
> *are the children of God. The Spirit you*
> *received does not make you slaves, so that*
> *you live in fear again; rather, the Spirit*
> *you received brought about your adoption*

> *to sonship. And by him, we cry, "Abba,*
> *Father." The Spirit himself testifies with*
> *our spirit that we are God's children. Now*
> *if we are children, then we are heirs—*
> *heirs of God and co-heirs with Christ, if*
> *indeed we share in his sufferings in order*
> *that we may also share in his glory."[38]*

We need to understand that adoption in that time period was different than how we view adoption in today's world. Most often, adoption is choosing a young child or infant to be brought into a family. That child lives with, and is raised as if they were the parents' own, biological kids.

Yet adoption in the first century was entirely different. They wouldn't often adopt children as we do. Instead, adoption was used to choose an heir to a family's inheritance. A child would be brought into the family for the sole purpose of continuing the family line.

In Paul's letter, we see that he spoke to the fact that we are brought into God's family not only to be adopted, but also to be heirs. Our adoption into God's family brings us so much more than we could ever imagine. Our inheritance is more significant than anything we can comprehend. Not only do we gain a fantastic inheritance, but we gain a greater gift: a loving, trusting, reliable Father.

For those people on this earth whose father has left them feeling disappointed, know that God is the one father whom we have always desired and needed and the one who will never betray us.

Once we understand our adoption, God will be a father to us. He will teach us how to walk in relationship with him. He will show us how his children behave and how dependable he is as our Heavenly Father.

My Father Story

Many of us have a unique story that either involves our dad or his absence from our lives. My father affected my view of God in different ways than your dad probably affected yours. This is the story of how my father impacted my view of God:

I know my father's presence in my life was a miracle in and of itself. My father taught me many different aspects of life while growing up. You can name the activity, and most likely my father taught me how to do it or at least something about it. He made it to many of my sporting events while growing up, and he was a huge supporter throughout my childhood.

However, my dad's loving and supporting presence in my life wasn't always the way of my childhood. You see, my father was less than perfect, as all dads are. Despite him being a good father, he had shortcomings that I now know affected my view of my Heavenly Father.

For years, due to my father's actions in my life, I believed that God didn't care, he was harsh and quick to anger, and enjoyed punishing me for my wrong decisions. I thought God only cared about me if I worked hard for him and that he didn't want me to live in peace.

One of the first ways my father affected my view of God was through his anger. I always felt as if he was angry at me. Whenever my sister or I wanted to do something and needed his permission, his first reaction was often anger. Each time we asked for something, he responded with outbursts, impatience, and irritation. Sometimes, he would verbally assault an idea until my sister and I simply felt stupid for asking. After he had some time to think an idea through, he eventually came around and granted permission to do what we had requested, and all was well. Yet it was that initial reaction of anger that taught me how to interact with my dad.

Eventually, I came to believe that God the Father would instantly be angry whenever I would ask him anything, too. So, just as I stopped asking my own father for anything, I wouldn't ask my Heavenly Father for things, either.

Can you imagine my surprise when I eventually read in Exodus 34, that God is compassionate, gracious, and slow to anger? I could hardly believe it. Then, I read in Matthew 7 of Jesus speaking about how our heavenly father gives us amazing gifts.

> *"Which of you, if your son asks for bread, will give him a stone? Or if he asks for a fish, will give him a snake? If you, then, though you are evil, know how to give good gifts to your children, how much more will your Father in heaven give good gifts to those who ask him!"[39]*

Years of believing that my Heavenly Father was angry had led me to miss out on the gifts he wanted to give me. He wanted me to walk in the truth that he is a good father who loves us and offers us amazing gifts.

The truth is that there is nothing we receive that doesn't come from him. All that is good comes from our Father. I started to realize that everything that has been given to me came from my Heavenly Father simply because he loves me.

It was and is still sometimes hard to believe, but this realization has had a significant impact on my faith and trust in my relationship with my Heavenly Father.

Performing

My father's most significant emphasis in my life was that he wanted me to succeed in whatever I did. He was always pushing me to be better at sports, academics, and extra-curricular activities. I believe that my dad's heart came from the right place, but he continued to push and prod me to exceed and excel.

This moved me into a place where I didn't believe that he would ever be proud enough of what I had accomplished. I felt as if I had to be the best at everything and relentlessly pursued my life to that aim. However, I continually came up short.

I recall one summer when I was playing in a baseball game, and I struck out at a significant point in the game. I could hear my father yelling at me from the crowd in the bleachers. Even though no one could see, I began to cry, knowing I'd let him down. As I walked into the dugout, I couldn't hold back. The small tears turned into a steady stream in front of some of my fellow players and friends. I 'lost it' due to the pressure I'd carried inside.

When my coach noticed, he came to comfort me. He told me I was trying too hard and needed to relax. I couldn't relax. How could I meet my father's expectation of me if I was just going to strike out? I found myself continually crumbling under the pressure to perform.

This pressure poured over into my relationship with my Heavenly Father as well. As I began a relationship with God, I always felt a pressure to perform for his love. I believed that I had to earn his love by my actions.

Not only are we unable to earn God's love, but our Heavenly Father also gives us affirmation and acceptance before we accomplish anything.

When Jesus was being baptized by John the Baptist, a voice from heaven came down and said, "This is my son in whom I am well pleased."[40] At this point in history, Jesus hadn't yet begun his public ministry. He hadn't turned water into wine, healed the sick and blind, fed five thousand people with a few fish, walked on water, or calmed a storm. All before he performed any miracles in the public eye, his father made it perfectly clear that he was proud of him.

God is proud of us even when we don't feel as if we are performing well enough for him. In fact, there is no pressure to perform for him at all. When we allow God to father us, he will show us his ways so that we can walk without fear of being rejected by him. God will teach us how to live in this world without any pressure to perform.

He wants to tell us how he sees us and how proud of us he is! All you need to do is stop long enough to listen.

I will never forget the day my earthly father told me that he was proud of me. It happened when I had told him about a book I wanted to begin writing. Returning to that moment in my head, I can remember the moment word-for-word.

At the time, I was struggling and stressed. Fundraising and ministry work had taken its toll. My phone rang, and I saw it was from my dad. I answered, and we talked briefly about what was going on in our lives. That's when he said it. "Garrett, I want you to know that I am proud of you, and I cannot wait to read your book!"

Hearing my father say he was proud of me felt so over-whelmingly encouraging that I was overtaken by emotion. Without hesitation, I began to sob.

When was the last time you heard your father tell you he was proud of you? I know some of you reading this may have never heard those words from a man's mouth, let alone your father. My heart breaks for you because I can't tell you how much these words are needed in so many people's hearts and lives.

God wants us to know that he is proud of us!

He wants to tell you, specifically, that he is proud of you. Here, I hope you will write your name in this blank and then read these lines out loud. Listen to God speaking this over your heart.

_____ , I am so very proud of you. You are my child in whom I am well pleased. I love you. You never have to earn or perform for my love. Child of mine, I just want to spend time with you!

Let these words of love sink into your heart and soul before moving onto the next section. You may need to say them as daily affirmations of who you are and how much God loves you.

Inconsistent

I never quite knew who was going to show up for me. Would it be the father who was happy with me? Or the one who was angry? Would he protect me? Or would he make sure I did things his way?

I was continuously left guessing how my father would react, and sadly, I was almost never right.

This emotional uncertainty poured into my relationship with God. Because of all of these mixed messages, I subconsciously believed that God was unpredictable, unreliable, and inconsistent.

However, God wasn't inconsistent, even though I had

assumed him to be. God, the Father, began to show me his unchanging nature and that he genuinely cared about me. This became one of the most significant truths in this relationship goal for me to learn.

Since then, he has become my strength and never been distant from me. He desires to be with me, and he is for me. Nothing can separate us from one other, or me from his love.

We can find all of these truths about God in scripture; truths about who God is and the relationship he wants to be in with us. I previously tried to build the truth of God outside of Scripture which caused me more harm. If our view of God is incompatible with what Scripture tells us, we will have a false view of who God truly is.

Simply put, we cannot form truth about him outside of God's inspired Word. And until I discovered this truth, I could not experience a complete and truthful view of God.

Absent

Many of you reading this chapter may say, "Well, at least you had a father." Perhaps you never had a father, or he left when you were young. What is important to understand is that the absence of a father in one's life will affect the way you view God. If this is your story, then you may believe that God the father doesn't want you or that he left you out to dry and doesn't care about you.

These are some of the lies that the enemy wants you to believe about your Heavenly Father. However, God is described as a father to the fatherless.[41] This is a fantastic description of who God is for those who do not have a father.

God is never absent from you. He doesn't leave you to make you live life alone. He wants you to know that he will never leave you or forsake you. He delights in who you are because you are his son, you are his daughter, and he takes pleasure in who you are.

If you have felt the pain of an absent father in your life, just remember Jesus knows the same pain. His father had to turn away from him while he took the sin of the world on his shoulders.

Jesus knows what it is like to feel the pain you are going through.

If you have experienced the absence of a father and are struggling, know that you have a mighty advocate in Jesus. He will always walk alongside you in your feelings of absence.

Jesus will lead us back toward God the Father, with whom he has an intimate relationship. We have to remember that nothing can separate us from the love of God. Even when we feel that he is absent from our lives, God is there working because of his love for us. God has a sincere desire to see those who have no father gain access to one.

Trust

Once again, trust is a massive aspect of another relationship goal. We will never have the relationship that God desires for us without a deep level of trust. In fact, we cannot have a relationship with God without trust.

God throughout scripture encourages people who are in a relationship with him to trust in him. He doesn't encourage this because he has failed us and we need to restore our trust in him. He does this because he is trustworthy.

Most children who have had a good father often have a deep level of trust in him. He is their protector. He is loving. A good father will serve as their strength and protection. A child who trusts in their father will follow him in obedience no matter what the father has asked of them, because he is trustworthy.

Many of us have been taught not to trust. The world has told us that no one is trustworthy. We have been told to trust no one until they have proven themselves worthy. Even then, we need to be sure to keep our guard up because you never know when they will stab you in the back.

God is more than willing to prove to you that he is a trustworthy Father. He will show himself to you and show you that he is the most trustworthy Father you could ever have. God's character alone proves to us that he is someone in whom we may safely and securely place our trust.

Ultimately, we as humans do have a sincere desire to trust. We are social creatures by nature, and we need intimate relationships. Are we then inherently designed to trust? I believe so. We were created to put our trust in others. However, here on Earth, we often fail to meet anyone in whom we can fully invest our unwavering trust.

We can't allow false beliefs or bad experiences to hold us back from putting our trust in the one who deserves it the most.

God the Father is the one in whom we can place our trust.

Innocence

As I grew in my relationship with the Father, I encountered a man who began to teach about growing in our relationship with God. On this particular day, he spoke about how God wants to return our innocence. I started to cry, realizing how the years of being influenced by the world had changed who I was and how I viewed life.

Jesus tells us that the enemy comes to steal, kill, and

destroy. This is precisely what had happened to my childlike innocence.

One of the best aspects of this fatherhood relationship goal is God's desire to restore our innocence to that of a child. That means no worrying and no anxiety, just pure faith.

God wants us to learn how to live in the innocence that we had as children. Remember Adam and Eve and the innocence they had while living in the garden? They didn't even know that they wore no clothes. However, the enemy robbed them of that innocence by prompting them to eat the fruit from the forbidden tree.

God wants us to be innocent like Adam and Eve before the fall.

When we walk in innocence, we cannot worry because we don't know how. We aren't fearful because all we know is that our Father will protect us. We aren't anxious because our Father's presence keeps us at peace. We aren't angry because we don't know what anger is. As we begin to have our innocence restored, we simply believe, as a child would, that our Father will take care of us.

When we walk in innocence, the world around us will take notice because we won't behave like the rest of the world. We stand out because we don't worry, we don't get anxious, and we don't have a lack of trust.

While the restoration process of God returning our innocence happens in an instant, learning to walk in innocence may take a lifetime. As we are learning there will be times when we will fall back into worry, anxiety, lack of trust, and lack of faith. The world around us will always try to take away our innocence. However, God's desire is for us to live in innocence.

If you're ready for God to return your innocence, simply ask God the Father now. Ask him, "Father, would you give me my innocence back? Would you teach me to walk as your child and walk in innocence?"

I believe that if you've just prayed that prayer, God has already returned to you your innocence. Just like that, God will restore in you the heart of an innocent child. Now go and learn how you are to live as a child of God.

8

MARRIAGE

Ephesians 5:31-32 NIV
"For this reason a man will leave his father and
mother and be united to his wife, and the two will
become one flesh. This is a profound mystery—but I
am talking about Christ and the church.

Singleness

Before we move deeper into this relationship goal, I want to speak to those of you who are single. If you are single, you've most likely been offended by the well-meaning Christian who has "tried" to help you with your singleness. Sometimes, this has caused more harm than good. I want to say that I am sorry if you have ever experienced this misfortune.

As I am married, I don't feel that I have much room to speak to the life of singleness. However, I do believe that God has given you a gift of singleness, and there is a great need to value that. There doesn't need to be an argument about which life is better: marriage or singleness. On the contrary, there should be a celebration for God's plan for our lives. As believers, sometimes we over-emphasize marriage over the importance of the 'marriage' we should have with Christ.

The fact you don't yet have a relationship like that doesn't mean that you are disqualified for God's marriage relationship goal. God has a great desire to speak to single people in this chapter about his love for you.

Do not let the fact that you are single hold you back from a relationship with God. He is your bridegroom. He relentlessly pursues you in an intimate relationship with him!

You are precious, you are desirable, you are wanted, and you are needed. You are not too picky, and there's nothing wrong with you. Remember, marriage on this earth is not the ultimate goal of our lives, even though we as Christians often make it out to be.

The point I hope you will walk away with from this chapter is that I believe our relationship with God may be the most intimate and most beautiful 'marriage' we will ever have.

I'm Just Dating Jesus

Have you ever heard a Christian say, "I'm just dating Jesus" when asked if they have a boyfriend/girlfriend? This happens when people choose to develop their relationship with God instead of dating someone on Earth at that time in their lives. The heart behind 'dating Jesus' is good as it often helps to prepare us for our future marriage.

However, the reality is that we are unable to date Jesus because the day we were saved was our wedding day with him. The 'dating' time was when he wooed us into a relationship with him.

If we genuinely want to learn how to be married in this

lifetime, then we should start with the marriage we have with Christ. What better way to learn how to date, how to be married, and how to walk in relationship with someone than through our relationship with him.

I believe that most of the time 'just dating Jesus' comes from a lack of knowledge that we are already married to him. However, there are also other reasons why we don't believe that we can have an intimate relationship with God in this relationship goal. The first is that we don't believe we are good enough. The second is because of the different fears that we have.

Unfortunately, many people never see the worth they have. They only see what is wrong and where they fall short. Because of this, it's easy to see why no one would ever want to be in a relationship with us.

Jesus didn't die so that you could continue to live your days on this Earth with a sense of unworthiness.

Such a feeling of not being good enough will actually restrict and keep us from diving deeper into a beautiful relationship with God. If we feel that we will never measure up and that no one will accept us for who we really are, then we are doomed to failure.

Nothing can separate us from his love.

Not even our own feelings of unworthiness or inadequacies.

Our fears have also kept us from experiencing real intimacy in this relationship with God. The first and most detrimental fear is the fear of commitment. Have you ever been around couples who have a huge fear of commitment? Their relationship is always on the edge of destruction because their fear controls their behaviors.

The world's view of marriage has tried to sell us the lie that we can be in a relationship without real commitment.

That you can have an intimate relationship yet keep your options open. This may have caused us to believe that we don't want to commit in case a better choice comes along, or maybe something or someone else would change our minds.

This fear also has a significant impact on our relationship with Jesus. We can't keep our options open and have an intimate marriage with Jesus. This relationship requires our full-fledged commitment to him and him alone. We cannot have real intimacy with God without real commitment behind it.

I have seen these fears also keep so many people who want a relationship with God out of one with him. "What will my parents think?" "If I believe in God, all of my friends will leave." "If I give my life to Christ, what will my spouse think about me?"

The fears that try to keep us from growing in an intimate relationship with God are endless. However, when we see the relationship that God wants and has planned for our lives, our fears will begin to melt away. When we look at Jesus for who he is, there will be no fear, and we will walk confidently into the relationship he has invited us into.

Marriage

Paul describes the beauty that can be found in marriage in Ephesians 5. As he ends this passage, he lets us in on what he is actually describing.

It is the relationship between Christ and the church.

This relationship goal reveals that Jesus is the groom and we are the bride. It tells us that Jesus is always pursuing us. He laid down his life for our relationship with him, exemplifying how marriage is about sacrifice, commitment, and love!

Marriage is an image that can be found throughout the Bible. Both the Old Testament and the New Testament have many references to our marital relationship with God. Why does God use marriage as a description of our relationship? Because it is the best depiction of intimacy in a relationship.

In marriages, spouses should know one other better than they know anyone else. In our world, there is no more magnificent description for, or example of, intimacy with God than the picture of marriage.

Unfortunately, our view of marriage today does not always match the picture God gave us in his Word. Many people no longer see the institution of marriage as a lifelong commitment between two people. Because of this false picture of marriage, there may be people who don't seek a 'marital' relationship with God. However, when we look at God's design not only for our worldly marriage but his marital relationship, we will see the beautiful, intimate, vibrant relationship we all desire to have.

The Ugliness of Unfaithfulness

One of my best friends in college found himself in a relationship with someone who sadly fell in love with someone else. While he wasn't married to this girl, he found himself dealing with the unfaithfulness of her actions. They were both in college, and he was working in the Rocky Mountains while doing an internship. It was while he was away that she fell in love with another man.

On a day that started out like any other, she called and said she was leaving him. My friend was devastated. He had no clue where he had gone wrong in their relationship and didn't know what would be next for him.

The next semester he returned to college to finish his school work. It was then that he felt God working through him, telling him to forgive his ex-girlfriend and reconcile their relationship. As he worked through the Lord's request, my friend began to experience the faithfulness of God in that relationship with her.

Despite the unfaithfulness they had experienced, through God's direction and my friend's willingness to listen, in time his relationship with her blossomed. In fact, the two even began to date again. They became engaged a year later and were soon married, and now they have a vibrant and healthy marriage.

Of course, this isn't the ending we are used to. It's probably one of the more unique times in which we actually see a couple 'stick it out', remain together, and stay in love.

In today's world, we see unfaithfulness in marriages and relationships all around us. Sadly, many people in the world have felt the sting of someone who has been unfaithful in a relationship. We are no longer shocked upon hearing about someone cheating on someone. Unfortunately, this is far too common in today's world.

Throughout the Bible, we see examples of God dealing with the unfaithfulness of his people. One of the most in-depth depictions of unfaithfulness to our marital relationship with God is found in the book of Hosea. In this book, we read how Hosea was prompted by God to marry a promiscuous woman named Gomer. Hosea did as God said and they were married and had a child together.

Then the story takes a drastic turn and for the worst. Gomer ends up leaving Hosea and falls back into promiscuity. She falls in love with another man and bears more children, none of whom are believed to belong to Hosea.

Hosea found himself in a similar position to my friend from college. God had told him, "Go, show your love to your wife again, though she is loved by another man and is an adulteress."[42]

In my mind, if I was in place of Hosea, I can imagine myself arguing with God about this. Do you not know what she did to me? Are you aware of what she is still doing?

Yet God goes on in Hosea 3 to say that Hosea is supposed to love Gomer as the Lord loved the Israelites, even though they turned to other gods. So Hosea went and bought her out of the slavery that she found herself in.

God used the story of Hosea and Gomer as a depiction of his love for the Israelites. Despite their rebellion, God was willing to rescue them out of their slavery and unfaithfulness to him.

God's love was and still is more significant than our mistakes and propensity to be unfaithful to our relationship with him. Fortunately for us, our lack of faithfulness has never nullified God's faithfulness to us.[43]

We will not encounter God outside of his faithfulness to us. Even when we have been unfaithful to our covenantal marriage with God, he restores us through his kindness. We have maybe been unfaithful to our relationship with God in more than one way, but he desires to restore us into an intimate relationship with him.

Newlyweds

My grandmother loves to watch game shows. We used to watch them together for hours when I visited her. Hollywood Squares, 21, Whammy, and several others were among her favorites. One show we would sometimes watch was called Newlyweds. This game show brought in people who were recently married. They were asked questions about one another while the other spouse was out of the room. The game was a test to see how much information they knew about their spouse even though they hadn't been married for long.

I am afraid that in some ways, as believers, we have turned Christianity into a newlywed game. We have turned our marital relationship with Christ into a knowledge-based relationship rather than a presence-based one. This happens when the goal of our walk with Christ has become to know more information about God rather than to walk with him.

If we turn our relationship into a newlywed game, we can make it look like we know all the right answers about Christ rather than having an intimate relationship with him. Our answers can come from rehearsed words rather than flowing out of our close relationship. The goal of our relationship with God is walking in an intimate relationship with him, not merely knowing answers about him.

I do believe God wants us to live as newlyweds with him in some regards. When we live as newlyweds, our relationship with him is always fresh, exciting, and adventurous. God's love and our relationship with him shouldn't become boring. The relationship with God that he has invited us into is the biggest adventure we could ever embark on. One where we can continuously learn more about who he is and our relationship with him.

We need to understand that this newlywed type of relationship is not based solely on feelings and emotions, but more on deep sacrificial love.

Love encompasses more than our emotions and feelings because there are many times when those internal feelings give us a false sense of what love truly is.

Love is based far more on the truth of who God is and his love for us than on our feelings about love. Our feelings and emotions will sometimes try and convince us that that the truth is not the truth, yet feelings have no influence on the truth.

God's love has deep and long-reaching effects! When we know and believe the truth, our emotions will line up with that truth. We will not only know we are loved, but we will feel loved by God.

Commitment

Have you ever met a couple who have been married for years, even decades, and are still blissfully happy together? We sometimes see them walking down the street, holding hands, and spending quality time together. They are kind to each other and treat each other with respect. These married couples remind us of newlyweds even though much time has passed since their wedding day. They have kept the fire of love kindled throughout their lifetime together.

This is part of the picture of the relationship Christ desires with us, where time doesn't quench our fire and intimacy with him but rather ignites it.

One of the most profound truths we will learn in this relationship goal is about commitment. That couple holding hands hasn't lost their first love and have lasted because of their commitment to each other. The same goes for our relationship with Christ. Love isn't just a fleeting feeling as much as it is a lifelong commitment. Our natural tendency as humans is to believe that love will eventually fade. This is because we have not based our definition of love on commitment.

We have been conditioned to move on to what's newer and better. We have seen this year-after-year, when millions of people line up as soon as the new iPhone is released. Despite having phones that work we are told that they are now outdated, and you are going to miss out if you don't upgrade.

Such a lifestyle has taught us nothing about commitment. In fact, it has shown us that we shouldn't commit for the long run but should only hold onto what we have until there is something better out there for us. We may very well live in the least committed generation that this world has ever seen. This truth has the potential to pour over into our relationship with others, and our relationship with God.

A few years ago, a couple whom I was listening to speak about marriage talked on this exact topic. When they were asked the key to sustaining a marriage, they gave a one-word answer. Commitment.

Commitment was the only answer to the question.

The couple went on to say that they grew up in a different world, one where you didn't throw things away when they broke or seemed 'old.' Times were different then, and people couldn't afford to replace items when they broke. This is the message that so many of us need to hear. It may take more time and more effort, but we can't afford to throw away what we already have in our lives.

Jesus came to restore our broken relationship with him. He came to Earth as the bridegroom for his bride so that we can have an intimate relationship with him. Jesus doesn't move on to the next thing when our relationship is broken. He is committed to fixing it.

In fact, he is the most committed member of our relationship. Jesus is so faithful to us that he died for us to begin and maintain our relationship with him. He shows us his commitment not only through his suffering on the cross but through the good, bad and ugly times of our lives.

He never leaves us and never forsakes us.

He is always there, no matter the circumstance because of his commitment to us.

Communication

If you ask married couples about the most essential aspect of their marriage, what do you think their answer would be? Usually, the response from married couples is good, open, and honest communication.

Communication is vital to relationships. Simply said, we cannot have healthy relationships without it nor can we experience the fullness of love if communication is absent. Communication is the gateway to intimacy. Without it, we are deadlocked outside of the close relationship that we are created for.

The truth is that we can't grow in our intimate relationship with God if we aren't communicating with him. It is the foundation on which we build a relationship with God.

If we are struggling in our communication with God, we may also falsely believe that he doesn't care about us after the relationship has begun. We have all heard the story about how a couple in which one spouse hasn't said I love you since the wedding day. Eventually, one of the spouses becomes frustrated before finally asking why the other spouse never voices the feelings of love for them. The spouse then usually responds with something like, 'Well I married you, didn't I?' Or, 'I said I love you when we got married, isn't that enough?'

There are times when communication becomes difficult that we can believe that God is that spouse who hasn't said I love you since the wedding day. If we fall into this trap, we may begin to think that God loves us enough to save us, but we don't believe that he loves us enough to want to spend every day with us. Know that Christ's death and resurrection means that eternal life begins here and now. We don't have to wait until heaven to begin that walk in intimacy with God.

Major roadblocks can interfere with our communication with God. Being too busy may be the greatest interruption. When we are too busy, we tend to ignore and skim over communicating with the people we love most. The world today may be the busiest time people have ever lived in. This only serves as a distraction to having intimacy with Jesus; it doesn't serve us or our relationship with him.

Have we become so concerned with this world that it gets in the way of our communication with him? We spend so much time on the computer, on cell phones, tablets, and may not be carving out time for him. Then we wonder why we haven't heard from God for a while and end up erroneously thinking he doesn't want to talk to us.

The truth is that we haven't carved out time for him.

One of the most significant aspects of healthy communication, one that often goes unnoticed in this busy world, is simply to stop and listen. We cannot properly communicate without listening. This is one of the most difficult aspects for us to learn in our relationship with God.

Some may feel that communication is a one-way street where we pray for hours without quieting ourselves and listening for a single minute. This may be one of the reasons why you haven't heard God in a while. It's not because he isn't trying to speak, but because you haven't taken the time to listen.

Admittedly, I also have a difficult time listening all of the time. In my marriage alone, this is one aspect of my shortcomings that causes conflict. Sometimes, I don't hear what Talia's saying, asking "What?", "Huh?", or asking her to repeat her words. Some could argue that I may need 'hearing aids,' and I probably wouldn't be the first husband about whom that was suggested.

My lack of listening is not due to lack of caring, but merely a lack of being in the moment and giving her and her words the fair time they deserve. Listening requires giving our full attention to the person who is trying to communicate with us. Our world isn't full of great listeners because we are constantly being tempted with distractions.

We all become frustrated when no one listens to us, but we also don't effectively listen to others when they are speaking. Listening may be one of the most overlooked and deteriorating arts in the world today.

Have we fallen into this same trap of busyness and are not taking time to listen to God?

God wants to communicate with us because he knows that we cannot grow in our intimacy with him without communication. He knows to establish and maintain intimacy we have to continue to communicate with him.

Conversations with God can start with simple questions. How was your day? What's on your heart? Then listening to what he says. Some days you will be amazed by what you hear and what you talk about. Other days, you may not hear much, and the conversations may seem rather ordinary. No relationships, and certainly no marriages, are built only on the extraordinary days. Quite the opposite, for most marriages are built slowly, over time, on the simple and the ordinary days, by people who are willing to communicate with one another.

We have covered a lot of ground in this chapter. We have seen that commitment and communication are essential to our intimacy with God. We have looked at the faithfulness of God and his desire to establish a marital relationship with him. No matter what you believe or where you are with God, you are ready to begin to walk in this relationship goal with him!

LORD AND KING

Revelation 19:16 NIV
On his robe and on his thigh he has this name written:
KING OF KINGS AND LORD OF LORDS.

Misunderstood

For believers, Lordship may be one of the most vital, yet most misunderstood aspects of a relationship with God. We may not understand Lordship because it is not familiar in our world today. To those who were Christians during Jesus' days, calling him Lord had many profound implications. Calling Christ Lord showed to whom they were ultimately allegiant. It impacted the way they walked on the earth and who was in charge of their lives.

We may have lost this relationship with God because while we love Jesus as our Savior, calling him, Lord has proven to be difficult. However, to call Jesus Savior and not call him Lord is something we cannot do.

We have also misunderstood the role of Jesus as our King. Some people in the world are no longer familiar with this type of leadership. Jesus is the King above all kings, and as believers, we are subject to his rule and reign on the earth. His kingdom is one that is unlike any kingdom we have seen on earth.

To many of you who have been calling and following Christ as King and Lord, these teachings may be somewhat simple. Remember that these chapters are simply introductions into who God is and the relationship that he desires for our life with him.

King

At the beginning of his life on earth, Jesus was worshipped as a king. In the early chapters of Matthew, we see that when Jesus was born, he was worshipped by men who had been awaiting his birth. Before he was even able to walk, before he could form words, he was revered as a king![44]

Throughout his years of ministry, Jesus told many parables about and proclaimed the good news of the kingdom of God. Jesus' kingdom is one that we can misunderstand in many ways if we don't carefully learn his teachings. Jesus was teaching the disciples, and he teaches us that our values must be based on heaven's values! He will teach us how to live under his authority in the kingdom of God.

Even in the final hours of Jesus' life before he was crucified, he was questioned by Pilate to find out his true identity!

> *"Pilate then went back inside the palace,*
> *summoned Jesus and asked him, 'Are you*
> *the king of the Jews?' 'Is that your own*
> *idea,' Jesus asked, 'Or did others talk to*
> *you about me?' 'Am I a Jew?' Pilate*
> *replied. 'Your own people and chief priests*

> *handed you over to me. What is it you have*
> *done?' Jesus said, 'My kingdom is not of*
> *this world. If it were, my servants would*
> *fight to prevent my arrest by the Jewish*
> *leaders. But now my kingdom is from*
> *another place.' 'You are a king, then!' said*
> *Pilate. Jesus answered, 'You say that I am*
> *a king. In fact, the reason I was born and*
> *came into the world is to testify to the*
> *truth. Everyone on the side of truth listens*
> *to me.'"[45]*

The beginning, middle, and end of Jesus' life were all centered on the fact that he was the King of the kingdom of God. Understanding this truth is the beginning of understanding our relationship with him. Learning to be in a relationship with the King will change how we view not only this world but our entire life.

Not a Tyrant

God does not use his supreme authority to control us. He uses it to serve us and foster the relationship only he can provide.

Despite this, we tend to believe, based on what we have experienced from controlling leadership in our world, that Jesus will want to control us.

God does not delight in having us under his thumb of control, but instead delights in being in a close relationship with us. When we understand this concept, his authority only serves to bring us into a more meaningful relationship.

In my travels overseas, I spent time in a closed country currently being led by a King. The history of the country boasts living under a monarchy's leadership for thousands of years. On one particular day, while traveling there, my tour guide took me to see where this king lived and ruled. I saw the palace from a distance, and the people with me told me all about their dearly loved king.

The stories about him were not about his rule and reign over his people. Instead, they told how the king was different from many of the kings who had come before him. He was kind and compassionate. He frequently did his own yard work, even though he had numerous servants paid to do so. He had a love for getting his hands dirty; something many kings before him had never done.

The people had fallen in love with their king. All around the country, he was adored. Not for the rules and regulations he had created, but for his seemingly ordinary attitude about life. He was relatable. Even though he had all authority in that country to do whatever he pleased, he modeled a service-minded mentality for his people. This king and ruler serves as a beautiful, worldly example of what good leadership looks like.

Likewise, we will fall in love with our ultimate King because of his love for us and his sacrificial leadership. As we continue to grow in our knowledge of his leadership, we will understand that he is not controlling but leading us towards freedom. When we submit to his leadership as our Lord and King, we will experience, perhaps for the first time, what loving authority honestly looks like.

Jesus is the King above all kings and the ruler over all nations, and he came down to earth to serve. Our King is not like any king we have or will ever come to know or serve under. While many of us have never lived under the rule and reign of a worldly king, we do live under the rule and reign of the King above all kings!

Rejection

If we aren't careful, we can end up rejecting Christ as our King just as Israel rejected God as their king in 1 Samuel.

> *"But when they said, 'Give us a king to lead us,' this displeased Samuel; so he prayed to the Lord. And the Lord told him: 'Listen to all that the people are saying to you; it is not you they have rejected, but they have rejected me as their king. As they have done from the day I brought them up out of Egypt until this day, forsaking me and serving other gods, so they are doing to you.'"[46]*

God gave them a king just as they desired, but as God had warned, it didn't turn out as they'd hoped. The nation of Israel had to learn the hard way that God was a better king and leader than anyone who could lead them on Earth.

The primary reason we see the nation of Israel rejecting God as their King is their desire to be like other nations.[47] Similarly, our world teaches us that being under the authority of someone else is the worst place for us to be. We are taught that we need to lead ourselves and be our own ruler. We want to be king of our own lives. Just like the nation of Israel, we want to look like the culture around us.

Our culture, perhaps more than any other in history, worships self-leadership and this is what we often desire. We want to be like the world around us, but this is not how God has created us to live.

While some may be genuinely in love with Jesus, and though we are thankful that he saved us from certain death, they may discard his leadership just as the Israelites did. Our desire to be like the people around us who have control overwhelms our desire to be ruled by the King above all kings. If the desire to be more like the world overtakes us, we will end up rejecting Christ as our King as well.

This dilemma is one of the primary reasons why I, personally fell away from my relationship with Christ. Those were years spent leading myself down a path of destruction. I discovered that my own leadership put me on a path I thought that I needed to be on. However, after so many years of the decisions I made on my own, many of which were wrong, I slowly began to understand that I needed someone else to lead me.

I needed God's leadership because when I was left on my own, I failed.

Just as God allowed the nation of Israel to have a king, God may let us be king in our own lives in some instances. He may do this only to prove that we are incapable of leading ourselves and in desperate need of a king, and that we were designed to live under the leadership of a king.

Even though many of us have at one point in time rejected Christ as our King, he will always give us the grace to restore our relationship with him.

He is the kindest King who will ever live.

His kindness restores us to the life Christ wants us to have, following him as our King!

Servant

When we walk in relationship with the Lord of Lords and King of Kings, we begin to learn how to live as a servant in the Kingdom of God. He teaches us how to walk as a servant even though it is entirely counterintuitive to the world we live in.

In Matthew 20 we see Jesus talking to his disciples about how we are called to be servants.

> *"Jesus called them together and said, 'You*
> *know that the rulers of the Gentiles lord it*
> *over them, and their high officials exercise*
> *authority over them. Not so with you.*
> *Instead, whoever wants to become great*
> *among you must be your servant, and*
> *whoever wants to be first must be your*
> *slave-- just as the Son of Man did not come*
> *to be served, but to serve, and to give his*
> *life as a ransom for many.'"[48]*

With this statement, Jesus essentially flipped the world's view of greatness. Our goal is not to work our way to the top, but instead to work our way to the bottom. Servants may hold the least status and recognition in the world's eyes, but in God's kingdom, they sit on the verge of greatness. The beginning of greatness in the kingdom happens through the obedience of a servant.

Being a servant of Christ is not something that is popular in our current day. The last thing we wish to do is serve someone else, and in fact, the opposite is often true, we want to be served. Some even believe we have a right to be served by others. This is a mentality that does not serve anyone well.

While Jesus is the King of kings, he does not use his place of royalty as an excuse to be served or waited on by others. The irony, of course, is that Jesus is the only one who has the right to be served by those around him. Instead, Jesus modeled what a true servant should look like by using the place and position he had been given to serve those around him.

As we learn through this relationship goal, we will begin to understand our role as a servant and that we were created not to be served but to serve others.

Intimate Lordship

In his Sermon on the Mount, Jesus makes the connection between him as Lord and knowing us in a close relationship.

> *"Not everyone who says to me, 'Lord, Lord,'*
> *will enter the kingdom of heaven, but only*
> *the one who does the will of my Father*
> *who is in heaven. Many will say to me on*
> *that day, 'Lord, Lord, did we not prophesy*
> *in your name and in your name drive out*
> *demons and in your name perform many*
> *miracles?' Then I will tell them plainly, 'I*
> *never knew you. Away from me, you*
> *evildoers!'"*[49]

There are times when we can separate what we do in our lives from our relationship with God. We can convince ourselves that we are walking in the will of God by doing righteous acts. However, without an intimate connection to Christ, we will still miss the point.

I once talked to a woman who after years of living in the church, realized that she still didn't have a real relationship with God. She'd grown up in the church, attended Sunday school, Wednesday night youth events, numerous summer camps, and even (for those who remember) *Acquire the Fire* events in Colorado. Her mother was also the worship leader of the church where her family attended.

After meeting with her, you would have thought that she was a fantastic believer. She was the picture-perfect believer in the mind of everyone around her. You would have never known that she didn't have a real and intimate relationship with God.

However, her relationship with God was based on accomplishing all the things she believed were good enough to get her into heaven. These accomplishments would have made you think that she not only had a relationship with God but had an amazing one.

Unfortunately, this story is the same story of countless other Christians. Their whole lives are lived in the church but they have missed out on an intimate relationship with Christ. The saddest part is that we may never know it's this way in their lives. The truth of the matter is that it is nearly impossible to develop intimacy with God in that type of performance-based relationship.

What Jesus says in Matthew 7 is not that we shouldn't serve or participate in the works of the kingdom. He isn't even saying that those aren't important. What he is saying is that it's not only what we do, but who we are with that counts.

There is another direction in which we can move away from Jesus' intimate Lordship. It is the exact opposite direction that we see him talking about in Matthew 7.

In John 14:15, Jesus tells the disciples that if they love him that they will do what he commands. Here is the connection we need to make: we cannot honestly say that we love and have a relationship with Jesus without being willing to obey his commands.

What Jesus is saying is that while we can make our relationship with him more about what we do, we also can't say we have a relationship with him if we don't do what he commands. When we say that we love him but are unwilling to do what he tells us, we end up rejecting his rule and reign in our lives.

Do you have an intimate relationship with Jesus as Lord? Have you found yourself fighting a temptation to work harder to earn a more intimate relationship with him? Or have you not been obeying what Jesus has commanded us to do? Either of these temptations often leads us directly away from the intimacy that Jesus desires us to have with him.

Boss

I vividly remember the night I gave my life to Christ. While being at the young age of four, my mom explained to me who Jesus was and what he did for me on the cross. She told me that Jesus died for all of our sins and was raised from the dead three days later.

She also went on to talk about the fact that Jesus is our Lord.

My mother obviously knew that the word Lord was not in my vocabulary at that age, so she proceeded to explain how Jesus was like a boss. She told me that Jesus would be in charge of my life and that I was supposed to follow him and his plan for my life.

I remember when I first confessed Jesus as Lord, I didn't fully understand the implications of that promise. And I'm sure I didn't fully understand the honor Jesus was due. But as

I have grown in my faith, I have come to understand it more and more.

This is how it works in relationship with God. As we continue to grow in our intimacy with God, we understand more of who he is.

If you find yourself struggling to compare the concept of Lordship to a boss, know that I'm not trying to lessen the definition of Lordship but instead build a bridge to deepen our understanding of it.

You may have even read about how we shouldn't use the term boss to describe Lordship. But for those of us who have lost sight of what Lordship is, we have to start somewhere. In many ways, this illustration does fall short, but I think it makes the term Lordship realistic in a way. Maybe this is where you need to begin your journey with Jesus as your Lord.

Note, though, that when we compare Lordship to a boss, we may have a tendency to lose the awe and reverence that should come with Lordship. Lord may be the most endearing and most exalted title that we can call Jesus and something the New Testament church would have called him. "To confess Jesus as Lord was to attribute to him authority and allegiance above all other authorities, rulers, or gods." [50]

Be Your Own Boss

One reason we reject Jesus as our Lord is that we want to be our own boss and leader. How many books have been written about how to start your own business and be your own boss? We as a human race crave this autonomy, and many loathe having to work for someone else and experience a lack of control.

I remember a story my aunt always told from my childhood. When I was little, we used to spend quality time with my aunt and, of course, she would tell me what to do. One day, I looked deep into her eyes, pointed at her with my little finger, and said to her that she was not the boss of me. Let me tell you, my comment did not go over well. I quickly figured out that my aunt was and could be my boss in a hurry.

Many of us have done this very thing in our relationship with God. We tell him that we love him because he died for our salvation, but we don't want him to boss us around. We most often reject his leadership because we desire to lead our own lives more than we trust God to guide us. Jesus can't take the wheel when we are trying so hard to drive. Some of us have never given Jesus control of our life because we want to be the one in charge.

Rejecting Lordship

In Mark 10, we see Jesus encountering a man who asks Jesus what he must do to inherit eternal life. Jesus told him to follow the commandments: you shall not commit adultery, covet, and several others. The man responded by proclaiming that he had kept all commandments since he was a boy.

Jesus told the man that he lacked one thing and that he needed to sell all of his possessions and give to the poor. After the man sold all that he had and gave to the poor, then he could return to follow Jesus. Being quite wealthy for those days, the man was quite sad. Because of the man's resistance, Jesus went on to say that it is difficult for the rich to enter the kingdom of God.[51]

So what was the issue with this man? Many blame the problem on his money, but the issue isn't money in itself. The problem was a Lordship problem. For the man was wealthy, and he'd allowed his wealth to rule him. If his wealth hadn't been controlling his life, he would have been able to give it all away and follow Christ.

Jesus asks us to get rid of anything that could become a 'lord' in place of him. For that wealthy man, money was controlling his life and was the one thing keeping him from following Jesus.

Is there anything in your life that is currently keeping you from allowing Jesus to be Lord?

We all are required to give up something when it comes to following Jesus, but this isn't a one-size-fits-all calling. Make no mistake that we need to give up anything that gets in the way of Jesus being our Lord. That means giving up whatever is leading us away or disconnecting us from the Lordship of Jesus.

The disciples provided us with an excellent example of what we are called to do when Jesus invites us into a relationship with him. When they were called by him to follow him and be fishers of men, they left their boats and nets behind. They dropped what they had known their whole lives in pursuit of an intimate relationship with Christ.

The disciples understood what it truly meant when they were asked to follow Jesus. The act required a complete change in the world in which they have been living. While we may never have to give up our occupation or give away all our wealth, our lives will truly change when we submit to the Lordship of Christ.

Loving Authority

I can remember a conversation I once had with my mother about the students in her class. Her response toward her students has always stayed with me.

She'd been struggling with the way that they were

behaving and acting in her classroom. My mom's heart broke over the disobedience she witnessed there. She knew, too, that it wasn't just in her class that students were not behaving like the people they should be.

While we were discussing her students, she told me this: "These kids are rebelling because they have never seen loving authority."

The lack of judgment or anger in that thoughtful and provocative statement was unbelievable. I'm sure my jaw must have hit the ground because I had never heard ill behavior addressed like that. Those kids were acting in rebellion because the only authority they had received was one not wrapped in love.

I guarantee we have all experienced authority that resembles this picture. Many of us have missed out on the beautiful picture of authority that comes out of a heart of love.

I believe a significant reason we have trouble submitting to the rule of Jesus Christ is that we have not experienced authority based in love. Authority outside of love is simply control. This is not how Jesus rolls.

Jesus will teach us how to live under his loving authority. He often talked about and modeled what it was like to live under this authority model. Jesus was willing to submit to his Father's authority because he understood that the Father knew what was best for him and loved him deeply.

When we understand that the authority given to Jesus is for our own good, we won't have a problem following him as our Lord and King.

SHEPHERD

John 10:1-5 NIV:
"Very truly I tell you Pharisees, anyone who does not enter the sheep pen by the gate, but climbs in by some other way, is a thief and a robber. The one who enters by the gate is the shepherd of the sheep. The gatekeeper opens the gate for him, and the sheep listen to his voice. He calls his own sheep by name and leads them out. When he has brought out all his own, he goes on ahead of them, and his sheep follow him because they know his voice. But they will never follow a stranger; in fact, they will run away from him because they do not recognize a stranger's voice."

Shepherd

In today's western world, we seem to have lost the symbolism that comes with God being a shepherd. Most people will live without ever seeing a sheep being led around by a shepherd in their lifetime.

Yet we see throughout scripture that God is depicted as

our shepherd. Not only throughout the Old Testament but also in the New Testament, as well. The prophet, Isaiah, clearly describes God as a shepherd.

> *"He tends his flock like a shepherd: He*
> *gathers the lambs in his arms and carries*
> *them close to his heart: he gently leads*
> *those that have young."* [52]

King David understood how God was his shepherd perhaps better than anyone else in his time period. He described God as our shepherd in Psalm 23. David speaks towards belonging to the shepherd and our contentment as his sheep. It is in these aspects of a relationship that many people in our world are missing, but God offers them to us in a relationship with him.

Jesus also spoke about shepherds and sheep when he was teaching people. He used these metaphors to point to our ultimate Shepherd: himself.

Lost Sheep

I remember a commercial a few years ago that grabbed my attention because of its uniqueness. In the opening segment of the commercial, you see a herd of sheep grazing on the side of a hill. In the middle of the herd, one sheep stands up on his back legs. He then looks around at the other sheep surrounding him and says, "Adios," then proceeds to walk out of the herd of sheep and out of the picture.

The commercial ends with a public message or encouragement to ditch the herd. To be your own person. Do things the way you want to do them.

This commercial is a depiction of how we as sheep can go astray.

We want to try to choose our own way. We want to be captain of our own ship. We don't want to be controlled, so we decide to walk away from what we were created for. We misunderstand the guidance, provision, protection, intimacy, and belonging that comes with a relationship with the Shepherd, and we walk away from the one thing we are seeking.

Our trust in ourselves may lead us astray because when we don't trust the Shepherd's guidance and leadership, we, in turn, go our separate ways. We become the "lead" sheep, believing we can lead ourselves and have no need of the Shepherd.

There are other times where we become lost, not due to our own rebellion, but because of small choices over time. We become lost not out of directly choosing to run away, but after a long line of decision-making that has led us away from the Shepherd.

In Luke 15 Jesus describes the shepherd who has lost a sheep and goes looking after it. No matter how we have become lost, Jesus is the Shepherd who goes after his lost sheep.

Jesus reminds us that when we have strayed away, not all is lost. We are valuable to God, and he wants to be with us. He desires to be the Shepherd of wayward sheep.

Jesus doesn't leave us to fend for ourselves.

He rescues us.

It's important to note that sheep have significant value in the shepherds' eyes. We are valuable to God. We aren't treated as objects or commodities. He doesn't use us. We aren't tradable or interchangeable.

No, God loves and values us because we are his.

We belong with the Shepherd!

Belonging

As we learn that Jesus is the good and true Shepherd, we will begin to live with a sense of belonging. This need is one of our deepest desires as humans. Belonging is not merely a want, but a necessity for us to flourish in life.

This concept should not surprise us as believers; we are hard-wired to desire to belong. Wouldn't it make sense that one of our deepest desires can be met through our relationship with God?

However, I believe many of us have wasted this deep urge to belong by searching in other places. Places that have left us feeling as if there is no place on this earth where we would fit in. If you have been like me, many of my years were spent trying to find the sweet spot of belonging. This expedition was an endless search and one that led to a whole lot of nothing.

Why? Only because I was looking in all the wrong places.

Note that I am not saying we can't find some sense of belonging through our relationships and groups on earth. I believe that God allows us to walk in belonging when we are walking with others that he has created us for. However, our sense of belonging may never truly be fulfilled until we are walking intimately with God.

We belong to Christ not because of anything we have done, but because he has paid the price for us. In the book, *A Shepherd Looks at Psalm 23*, the author looks at belonging in a way that most of us may not be familiar with.

> "I recall quite clearly how in my first venture with sheep, the question of paying a price for my ewes (female sheep) was so terribly important. They belonged to me only by virtue of the fact that I paid hard cash for them. It was

money earned by the blood and sweat and tears drawn from my own body during the desperate and grinding years of the Depression.

And when I bought them that first small flock, I was buying them literally with my own body which had been laid down with days in mind. Because of this, I felt in a special way that they were in very truth a part of me and I a part of them. There was an intimate identity involved which, though not apparent on the surface to the casual observer, nonetheless made those thirty ewes exceedingly precious to me."[53]

This is precisely the depiction that Christ made when he paid for us on the cross. Isaiah describes this very thing in Isaiah 53.

> *"We all, like sheep, have gone astray, each of us has turned to our own way; and the Lord has laid on him the iniquity of us all."[54]*

Despite our propensity to walk away from our shepherd, he took our iniquity on himself. He cared so much for us that he was willing to lay down his own life for us. In order for us to be with him.

When we are with the Shepherd, we cultivate this sense of belonging.

His presence is the cure for our lack of encountering meaningful belonging here on earth. God has developed this sense in us because, ultimately, this is what we were created for.

We belong in his presence.

Listening

Hearing God's voice is a vital component in this relationship goal with God. God is not mute, and we aren't incapable of understanding his voice. To truly hear God, we need to be in close proximity to him to listen to his voice.

If we distance ourselves from God, then we will have a difficult time hearing his voice. Hearing our Shepherd doesn't come through trying to listen to him; it comes through being close to him, knowing his voice, and spending time in his Word.

We see Jesus speaking the fact that his sheep know his voice and listen to him in John 10.

> *"The gatekeeper opens the gate for him, and the sheep listen to his voice. He calls his own sheep by name and leads them out. When he has brought out all his own, he goes on ahead of them, and his sheep follow him because they know his voice."*[55]

If we aren't listening to our Shepherd, then we will lose all sense of direction and possibly even lose sight of where we are supposed to be. Not because the Shepherd doesn't care, but because we're too far from his presence. This happens to sheep, creatures that are in desperate need of a shepherd's guidance and leading. If we distance ourselves too far from the shepherd, our lives will wind down a path we weren't designed to be on.

There are times where we do not submit well to the direction and voice of our Shepherd. This may lead to us having difficulty hearing God's voice. A. W. Tozer tells us that "most Christians don't hear God's voice because we've already decided we aren't going to do what he says." If we are having difficulty hearing God, we may need to check our heart to make sure that we haven't fallen into this trap.

There will be times where we are tempted not listen to our Shepherd. If we know we're not going to do what the Shepherd says, then we will have a hard time hearing his voice.

What we need to understand is that the words of the Shepherd lead to life. We need to remember from Jesus' words that the reason that he came was so we can have life and live that life to the fullest. When we hear the Shepherd's voice and walk in his obedience, we will always walk into life and abundance.

The voice of God leads us into the life we are designed to live in because he cares for us and he knows what is best.

Knowing His Voice

One truth we need to understand in this relationship goal with our Shepherd is the sheep recognize and know his voice. To know his voice takes time and intimate knowledge of our Shepherd. As we spend time with the Shepherd, we will become more familiar with his voice.

Understand that we are always learning, and our shepherd gives us time to learn his voice. He doesn't expect us to get it right the first time, and he doesn't get angry when we fail to recognize his voice during this learning process. He allows us time to walk through an understanding of who he is and how we can realize it is him.

Early on in my dating relationship, Talia would often give the phone to someone else and try to trick me into believing it was her. When we first started dating there were several times when I was fooled. However, as we continued dating, I became more and more familiar with the unique tone and sound of her voice. Eventually, when she gave the phone to another, I immediately knew it was not her, and the game ended.

This is precisely how we learn our Shepherd's voice; by spending time with him and developing trust in his voice.

The Thief

Jesus says we will know and be able to tell the difference between him and the thief because we won't recognize the other voice.[56] This is yet another reason that our Shepherd will continue to teach us his voice through this relationship goal. Not only to follow and have an intimate relationship with him, but also so we will recognize when the thief comes.

One reason we can get swept away from Jesus is by mistaking an imposter's voice for that of the Shepherd. The thief that comes to steal and kill the sheep will try to imitate the Shepherd's voice to fool us. Our knowledge of our Shepherd's voice will guard us against any deception. The only way we know the difference is by recognizing and knowing the Shepherd's voice.

The thief often tries to come in as an imposter. We will know him because he does not come in as the shepherd, nor does he act like the shepherd, or speak like our Shepherd.

That which leads to death is the way of the thief.

Those who follow the good Shepherd follow the path that leads to life.

Any voice that leads us towards destruction is the voice of the thief. He comes to steal, kill, and destroy. His mission is to separate us from our Shepherd and separate us from the life we are designed to live. Being able to discern between the Shepherd and the thief is vital to our survival. We will never fall into following the thief when we are in close relationship with the Shepherd.

Hard Time Hearing

Admittedly, not being able to hear God's voice is one of the greatest frustrations that comes with our walk with God. Sometimes, it may seem as if we are out of cell service in the middle of nowhere, feeling alone on our search to hear God. We know we need to hear God, yet so many times we just can't seem to connect with him.

Have you ever had difficulty hearing God's voice? I have. In fact, I've walked through several seasons of my life when it seemed as if I couldn't hear God despite my best efforts.

When we don't hear God, over time we tend to develop a bad theology about him. We begin to believe that God is something he is not or that we have done something to offend him, so he gives us the silent treatment.

We need to continue to believe that God is God and he is good even when we aren't hearing him or hearing clearly. He is the same today, tomorrow, and for all eternity. Our lack of hearing him won't change who he is. It is too easy to become frustrated when we are in this place, and we may start to believe false things.

Let us not fall into this place, no matter how difficult the season we are in is. Do not alter your beliefs because of your difficulty in hearing him.

Instead, step closer into his desire for a relationship with you.

And when you are there, stop and listen.

"Try not. Do or do not. There is no try." – Yoda

Perhaps many of us could benefit from Yoda's encouraging words, spoken to a young Jedi in training.

There is no 'try' in listening to God's voice. For the countless days and weeks that I have "tried" to hear the voice of God, you would think that I would have this skill mastered. Honestly, I don't. This skill is a process, one that involves learning and patience to come to a place where we know it is not our own effort that makes God speak.

So what do I mean by 'there is no trying' in hearing God's voice? This statement means that we cannot force, coerce, or manipulate God into speaking to us. Nothing we do in our own strength will get us to a place where we can hear the voice of God. In fact, when we are striving too hard to hear God's voice, it often means we are doing it out of our own efforts and strength. For no amount of effort can force God into speaking to us.

Ultimately, hearing God's voice is much more about our submission to him than it is about our efforts to hear him. When we submit to his voice, we are saying that we are ready to hear whatever he has to say, when he has to say it.

Worried Sheep

"The Lord is my shepherd, I lack nothing."[57]

Is this your heart's cry? I lack nothing, or I shall not want? I believe God will create in our hearts a sincere desire to walk in this world in contentment. We aren't actually designed for a constant craving for something more or better. Our constant desire for more is what steals our joy in the moment.

Being content is something far-fetched and undervalued in our society. We are told in our world that we can continuously want more and want those desires to be fulfilled immediately. Can you ever remember a time on Christmas Day, where you saw someone as they opened a gift be filled with joy? Then, when the next gift was opened, that joy turned into envy? This is what happens when we walk in discontentment. Our desire for more leaves us in a place centered on comparison, not contentment.

Our constant comparison will always kill our contentment. But our Shepherd will teach us how to be content in all circumstances, no matter what anyone has or accomplishes around us.

I believe that God wants to take away our capacity not only to compare but also to worry. Have you ever seen a worried-looking sheep? While I have seen scared sheep, I have never seen a sheep who is living in a constant state of worry. Sheep don't have the capacity to worry like we do as humans.

Our worry comes from a place that lacks contentment and struggles with comparison. Our worry also comes from a place of not truly understanding who God is.

Our Shepherd is our provider.

Our Shepherd is our protector.

We don't need to worry because he knows what we need before we even need it.

While I've never seen a worried sheep, I have seen countless Christians who live in a constant state of worry. They are Christians who have fallen out of being shepherded by God. When we worry, we are not trusting that we have a good Shepherd who cares about our well-being.

Sheep who don't trust their shepherd don't end up gaining access to the abundant blessings he provides. They also don't trust in the protection the shepherd provides. The safest place for us to live is under the protection and provision of our Shepherd.

What if the only concern we had was being close to the

Shepherd, trusting that he knows what is best for our life as a sheep? What if all we were concerned about, was following the shepherd's voice and walking in obedience? It is when we focus on our relationship with the Shepherd and his desires that he gives us contentment in our current circumstances.

When we are close to the shepherd, we have no reason to worry because we know who he is.

Learning to live without worry and in contentment takes time to learn. Remember the Israelites in the desert who believed they were going to die because of a lack of water? We usually jump on their actions and say, "But didn't you know who God was?" Or we say, "He just rescued you out of slavery, and still, you're worried about him providing your food?" The Israelites weren't living in a sense of contentment in their circumstances even though they'd always lived in a lack of abundance before they were rescued by God.

God was preparing them for the promised land. On the way, he tried to teach them both contentment and trust. If we cannot learn how to live in the desert seasons with God, we will be incapable of thriving in the promised land. If we can trust God in the desert, then we will trust God in the promised land.

Despite all of our circumstances, God will teach us how to not live in a constant state of worry and want. Thankfully, we have a loving Shepherd and one who is willing to teach us how to live in a place of contentment in every circumstance we may face.

RABBI

Mark 1:16-18 NIV
"As Jesus walked beside the Sea of Galilee, he saw
Simon and his brother Andrew casting a net into the
lake, for they were fisherman. "Come, follow me,"
Jesus said, "and I will send you out to fish for
people." At once they left their nets and followed
him."

Follow Me

Come follow me. At once the disciples dropped their nets.

We are often convicted by seeing these disciples dropping their nets immediately. Why did they do this without any question or regard for their former life? Joseph Stowell answers this in his book, *Following Christ*.

"If you had been Thomas or Peter or any other disciple and you believed that this was the One who had finally come to fulfill all your inner longings and establish stability in your world, you may have left your nets as well. If you had heard the incarnate God of the universe call you face-to-face, you would have impulsively obeyed. That word "Me" in His call to "Follow Me" is what makes unconditional followership so compelling."[58]

When we come face-to-face with Jesus, the calling is overwhelmingly compelling. When we are face-to-face with the one who can and will fulfill all of our longings, it doesn't take but a second to think about following him. We immediately follow him because of who is calling us into a relationship.

However, not every disciple responded in this way upon hearing that Jesus was the Messiah. We see this in the calling of Nathanael. Nathanael was at first a skeptic when he heard from his friend that they had found the Messiah.

Right after Philip began to follow Jesus, he went to find his friend Nathanael. We find this story in John 1.

> *"Philip found Nathanael and told him, 'We have found the one Moses wrote about in the Law, and about whom the prophets also wrote--Jesus of Nazareth, the son of Joseph.'*
> *'Nazareth! Can anything good come from there?' Nathanael asked.*
> *'Come and see,' said Philip.*
> *When Jesus saw Nathanael approaching, he said of him, 'Here truly is an Israelite in whom there is no deceit.'*
> *'How do you know me?' Nathanael asked.*
> *Jesus answered, 'I saw you while you were still under the fig tree before Philip called you.'*

> *Then Nathanael declared, 'Rabbi, you are the*
> *Son of God; you are the king of Israel.'"[59]*

Some people have a tendency to use Nathanael as a punching bag. These people often use him as an example of how you should not treat the call of Jesus to follow him. Nathanael had difficulty believing that anything good could come out of the little town of Nazareth. Despite his grave concerns about this man, Nathanael went to check it out.

Nathanael's doubt didn't keep him from getting close to Jesus to see if he was the real deal. Nathanael just wanted to know that Jesus was who he said he was. He most certainly had heard about men making claims that they were the Messiah who had come to deliver Israel from their enemies before Jesus' time. He had his doubts about his friends' remarks that Jesus was the one whom Moses and the prophets wrote about.

Nathanael wasn't willing to give his life to someone who wasn't the true Messiah.

Jesus didn't treat Nathanael with contempt because he had doubts about him. In fact, Jesus did the exact opposite. Jesus forgoes all his unbelief and doubts and aimed straight at his heart. He did this by telling Nathanael that he knew precisely who Nathanael was and where he was before he came to see him. I can't imagine the shock on Nathanael's face upon hearing those words from Jesus.

Jesus' words struck a chord immediately in Nathanael's heart. He instantly trusted that Jesus was who he said he was.

Many of you may have heard the calling of Jesus and dropped your nets immediately as some of the disciples did. But for those who are struggling and doubting that Jesus is who he says, know that his invitation is not only to follow but also to come and see.

Jesus will show you that he is who he says he is, and when you accept the invitation to come and see, don't be surprised if it leads to you quickly saying, "Rabbi, you are the Son of God; you are the king of Israel."[60]

Cost Of Discipleship

In today's world, the message of the cost of discipleship is not popular in many Christian circles. However, Jesus did not seem to shy away from the concept of the cost of disciple-ship. This isn't something that Jesus mentioned only once. He actually spoke of it several times. Jesus wants us to know that to truly follow him, it will take everything you have.

> *"Large crowds were traveling with Jesus.*
> *Turning to them, he said, "If anyone comes*
> *to me and does not hate father and mother,*
> *wife and children, brothers and sisters--*
> *yes, even their own life--such a person*
> *cannot be my disciple. And whoever does*
> *not carry their cross and follow me cannot*
> *be my disciple. "Suppose one of you wants*
> *to build a tower. Won't you first sit down*
> *and estimate the cost to see if you have*
> *enough money to complete it? For if you*
> *lay the foundation and are not able to*
> *finish it, everyone who sees it will ridicule*
> *you, saying, 'This person began to build*
> *and wasn't able to finish.' "Or suppose a*
> *king is about to go to war against another*
> *king. Won't he first sit down and consider*
> *whether he is able with ten thousand men*
> *to oppose the one coming against him with*

twenty thousand? If he is not able, he will send a delegation while the other is still a long way off and will ask for terms of peace. In the same way, those of you who do not give up everything you have cannot be my disciples."[61]

Jesus compares the cost of discipleship to carrying his cross. Jesus tells the people following him that they must pick up their cross to do so.

This means that to follow Christ, we must die to our wants and desires for his. This death is actually a beautiful one because once we lay down our wishes and desires, Christ will replace them with his.

To some, this may seem as if it's not worth the cost, but remember that God knows our wants and desires more than we know ourselves. While we may think we would be losing out on something, the truth is that we gain so much more than we ever could have if we choose not to follow Jesus.

No one can escape the cost of following Jesus.

When we are confronted with following Jesus, he will point to what is holding each of us back from following him.

We must realize, the 'net' we are holding onto is different for everyone. The rich man who came into contact with Jesus was asked to give up his possessions. Others were asked to leave family members behind. The disciples themselves each had to give up different things: fishing, collecting taxes (which was then quite a lucrative business), and various other occupations. God may ask you to leave your way of life to follow him entirely.

This is the exact circumstance I fell into when Jesus asked me to follow him. I had to give up what I had spent my entire life pursuing: taking over my family's multimillion-dollar farm.

For others, when Jesus asks them to follow him, it doesn't always mean they will have to quit their job or pursuit of a career. Their net may be the pursuit of money or position in their field. While their job may not change, Jesus will change and revolutionize the way they view their role.

When Jesus calls us into a relationship, we are confronted with the 'net' that we are holding in our hand. The disciples chose to drop their nets to follow Christ. They knew they needed to let go of their past and walk into the present to follow Jesus.

Are you ready to drop whatever net you have in your hand in order to follow Jesus?

Cost of Non-discipleship

When we are confronted with the cost of discipleship, we can be overwhelmed by what it is going to cost us. When this happens to us, we must remember what it cost Jesus to be on the cross: his life. Is what we have to give up more than what he gave? What we have to give through our pursuit of following God will never outweigh what Jesus gave.

There is also another cost we must consider when we are confronted with the call to be Jesus' disciple. It is the cost of not following him. The cost of non-discipleship.

When we are confronted with the cost of discipleship, we almost never compare it to the cost of not following Jesus, yet shouldn't we weigh both equally?

What will we miss out on if we have chosen not to follow Jesus?

Much more than we can afford.

Remember the rich man who asked Jesus what he needed to do to inherit eternal life? When he was confronted with the cost of discipleship, it didn't add up in his mind. We do know that he wasn't willing to give up all of his wealth to follow Jesus. What we don't know is if he ever considered what he would have to give up if he didn't follow Jesus.

What did the rich young ruler miss out on?

What was his cost of not following Jesus?

The rich man missed out on a life filled with hope, love, joy, and peace. Most importantly, he will miss out on being forgiven of all his sins and walking into an intimate relationship with God for eternity. His decision means that he will forever miss out on having true fellowship with God, and he will never know the joy of following God and walking in a life of abundance that only God can give.

The costs of not following Jesus can go on and on, but when we say no to following him, the ultimate cost is missing out on the relationship he has invited us into.

Intimate Teacher

I was always puzzled by the passage in John 1, where John the Baptist encounters Jesus for the first time in person. Two of John's disciples after this encounter leave John to follow Jesus. When Jesus discovered they were following him, he turned and asked what they wanted.

They asked, "Rabbi, where are you staying?"

What kind of response is this? Where are you staying? I was utterly dumbfounded by this question and by Jesus' answer. He responded, "come, and you will see!" So that was precisely what they did; they began to follow Jesus.

When we understand what discipleship looked like in the

first century, we understand why they asked Jesus that question. It was because they were serious about being his disciples.

We may have a hard time understanding the relationship between a rabbi and his disciples. When we read about the disciples following Jesus, we tend to skim over these passages. When we think of teachers or rabbis, we often think of going to school for long hours each day for specific months of the year. This was not how teaching and discipleship happened in the first century.

Following a rabbi was much different than what we typically think of when being taught by a teacher. It was more about literally following him. Disciples followed him, lived with them, and imitated their rabbis. They learned not only from what their rabbi said, but also by what they did, and how they reacted to everyday life as well as how they lived.[62]

A Jewish historian once explained, a disciple would not "grasp the full significance of his teachers learning in all its nuances except through prolonged intimacy with his teacher."[63] Prolonged intimacy. This is the goal of being in a relationship with our Rabbi. In fact, it is the goal of every relationship goal: intimacy with God. When considering the purpose of our teacher, will we completely miss the point if we try to achieve anything other than intimacy.

The goal of Jesus' teaching was to lead his disciples closer to him.

We must go where he goes.

Sleep where he sleeps.

Learn from his life.

Only then will we learn how to be taught through circumstances while being with him. He can and will show us how to walk through whatever situations we face in life.

The goal is prolonged intimacy with our Rabbi.

Learning From Our Rabbi

I love the picture we see of Jesus while working with his disciples. He was out in the towns, healing people and proclaiming the good news about the kingdom of God. It was an amazing learning experience for the disciples as they learned from their Rabbi not only how to teach but how to live life as his disciples.

> "Along with instructing the crowds, a rabbi's greatest goal was to raise up disciples who would carry on his teaching...
> A disciple apprenticed himself to a rabbi because the rabbi had saturated his life with Scripture and had become a true follower of God. The disciple sought to study the text, not only of Scripture but of the rabbi's life, for it was there that he would learn how to live out the Torah. Even more than acquiring his master's knowledge, he wanted to acquire his master's character."[64]

This is the goal of our Rabbi: not only prolonged intimacy with him, but also that we would carry on his teaching and lifestyle.

The descriptions of the disciples should give us a clue about the type of men being taught by Jesus. From arguing about who is the greatest, to being afraid of dying in a storm on the sea. The disciples were a rough and rowdy crew with twisted agendas. They had wrong beliefs, were quick to judge, and they tried to keep people away from Jesus.

Peter was compulsive.

Thomas was a doubter.

Two of Jesus' disciples were named the sons of thunder.

Yet these are the men that he chose who would transform

into the men who would flip the world upside down after living and learning for three years with him.

This transformation of the disciples gives us a picture of what can happen as we learn from our Rabbi. No matter who we are and where we start, we will become the person God has created us to be as we learn from him.

As we read about Jesus' life it is amazing to see how Jesus changed people's lives in an instant, but I wonder if the disciples ever became frustrated with him. They were constantly seeing how he had changed some people's lives in an instant, while in their own lives it oftentimes was a much longer process.

Sometimes, we can become so wrapped up in the thought that God isn't doing something in an instant that we miss what he is trying to teach us. What he may do in an instant in someone else's life, may take us years to go through. In these moments, we have to trust that our teacher knows what is best for our lives. We also have to remember what the ultimate goal of our Rabbi is: prolonged intimacy.

As we read in the gospels, it was a three-year process for the disciples to learn and understand Jesus, but he wasn't done with them after he left Earth. He then gave the Holy Spirit as a teacher. He'd told the disciples that the Holy Spirit would teach them and remind them what he has already taught.

Today, two thousand years after, Jesus is still our teacher through the power of the Holy Spirit.

Our Rabbi is still teaching us today.

Know that we are more than likely going to fail at following Jesus as our Rabbi at some point in time. Even the first disciples had moments of failure. We must learn to handle our failures, but we don't have to do so alone. Our Rabbi will teach us through our failures.

We need to understand that Jesus is the most patient teacher we will ever learn from. God is so gracious with us in the midst of our failures. We are often harder on ourselves than Jesus is on us. In fact, even when we don't have grace for our own mistakes, he still gives it to us.

I absolutely love the moment we get to see when Jesus talks to Peter about his failure in abandoning and rejecting him after Jesus was crucified. We find this encounter in John 21.

After the death of Jesus, the disciples had returned to their boats once again. They were fishing when a man yelled at them from shore and commanded them to throw their nets on the other side of the boat. While this was ridiculously difficult to do, they followed what the 'stranger' had said. As a result, the net filled up so quickly, that they were unable to haul it into the boat.

Peter instantly knew it was Jesus who had spoken to them. He immediately jumped from the boat and began to swim to the shore. He couldn't wait to get to Jesus, so he jumped ship to get to him faster.

Despite his failure and the short amount of time between, Peter still wanted to be with Jesus. Peter's desire to be with Jesus overrode any feelings from his failure. Most of us would have probably stayed in the boat, not wanting to face or own up to our failure.

In this encounter, Jesus didn't ignore the fact that Peter had failed, but he also didn't condemn him for it. Most of the time, when we fail, we believe that Jesus may point out our failure, and rub it in our faces. This couldn't be farther from the truth. Jesus' heart is set on restoration. Peter's failure didn't disqualify him from running to Jesus or his purpose. Despite Peter's failure, Jesus restores Peter to his original destiny.

We can't learn from our failures if we aren't close to our Rabbi. When we fail, we have to run back to Jesus. He is the only one who can restore us back to a relationship with him and to our destiny.

Amazing Authority

As we talk about Jesus being our rabbi and our teacher, we have a tendency to strip Jesus of his divinity. Jesus isn't simply a teacher or rabbi, but he is the greatest teacher and the greatest rabbi who has ever walked the earth.

There is nothing ordinary about Jesus.

He is God in the flesh, and he calls us to be his disciples.

When we begin to follow Jesus, we will see Jesus as decidedly different from any other teacher we could know. Jesus taught as one who had authority, not as the teachers of the law.

Jesus used his authority to bring people into a closer relationship with him and the father. Jesus also used his authority to teach people how to serve and love others.

He didn't use it to lord over us or control us, but rather to teach us how to walk on this earth.

In Mark 1 and in John 7 we see another group of people encountering Jesus' amazing authority.

> *"They went to Capernaum, and when the*
> *Sabbath came, Jesus went into the*
> *synagogue and began to teach. The people*
> *were amazed at his teaching, because he*
> *taught them as one who had authority, not*
> *as the teachers of the law."*[65]

> *"Not until halfway through the festival did*

*Jesus go up to the temple courts and begin
to teach. The Jews there were amazed and
asked, "How did this man get such
learning without having been taught?"
Jesus answered, "My teaching is not my
own. It comes from the one who sent me."[66]*

We have never and will never experience anything greater than the teaching that comes from our Rabbi. As we walk with him, we will often live with a sense of amazement in the authority of Jesus. In both Mark 1 and John 7, the people surrounding Jesus were amazed by his authority and teaching. However, we don't know or see if these people follow Jesus after encountering him. If we aren't careful, we can be in awe of the authority of Jesus but miss the relationship he is calling us into.

The awe and amazement we experience in the authority of Jesus is designed to lead us closer to him. However, we live in a world that moves onto the next amazing thing at the speed of light. We have been conditioned to move onto whatever causes us to "ooh" and "ahh" next. As we walk with Jesus, we must not move beyond living with a sense of awe and wonder in who he is and his teaching. The purpose of Jesus' authority and teaching is to bring us into an intimate relationship with him as our Rabbi.

12

PROMISES

Numbers 23:19 NIV
God is not human, that he should lie,
Not a human being, that he should change his mind.
Does he speak then not act?
Does he promise and not fulfill?

Promises

The Bible is full of promises for God's people. We see promises or the fulfillment of God's promises in nearly every book of the Bible. God uses promises in mighty ways to teach us how to walk in relationship with him. He also uses promises to show us his desire for a relationship. His promises show us parts of his character that we would not see outside of those promises.

One of the promises we will use as a reference throughout this chapter is the promise that God gave to Abram. If you aren't familiar with that name, it is because most of the time we refer to him as Abraham. Abram was his name before

God changed it to Abraham. God's promise to Abram was that he was going to be the father of an entire nation.[67] God's promise wasn't just to bless him, it also was designed to draw him into a deeper relationship with God. We will see how God's promise to Abraham helped develop a deeper relationship with God and how God's promises can help us walk in a deeper relationship with him as well. Before we do that, though, let's look at how we view and interact with promises today.

Broken Promises

I can remember a day where pinky promises were almost admissible in court. Back in third grade, if you made a pinky promise to someone, that meant your promise had to be good. However, in today's world, we almost treat the word 'promise' as if it's a four-letter word. It is not something that we want to hear from people for fear that their promise may never come true.

When did we lose our sense of trust in people's promises? I believe it comes from the fact that we have seen too many broken promises in our lives to trust other people's promises implicitly.

Unfortunately, we have projected these same sinful human promises, onto those promises that come from God.

Many, if not all of us, have encountered promises that have been broken by people. For the majority of us who have been in places where promises were broken, we cannot allow that to influence and impact the promises that God has designed for our lives. Regardless of our worldly experiences and disappointments, God desires us to walk into the promises he has ordained.

Unlike people on earth, God has never failed to come

through on a promise he has made. He is the ultimate promise-maker and promise-keeper. His word never fails and never returns void.[68]

Furthermore, when we see the promises of God not come to fruition in one person's life, they almost always eventually come true in another generation. God's promises stand the test of time. Thousands of years can't stop them. Take a moment to think about that. Long after your life here on Earth, God's promises will still be brought to fruition in people's lives.

His promises are as eternal as he is!

Sometimes, we believe that God makes good on promises to others, but not to us. Or that God shows up for other people's lives, but when it comes to our own relationship with him we're not sure he will. We may have developed this thought process because we can more clearly see God working in others' lives than we can see him working in our own.

We have built our beliefs about God based on the snapshot that we see in other people's lives, not on who God actually is and what the Word of God says. This is what I refer to as comparative theology. We base what we believe about God and who he is, off of what he doesn't do in our lives compared to what he does in others.

However, God's work in our lives won't always look like it will in other people's lives. Our journey with God is uniquely designed for us. The enemy loves to grab our attention by trying to get us to compare our lives with others. We cannot fall into this trap of comparison if we want to fully engage God's promises for our lives.

Too Good To Be True

If it sounds too good to be true, then it probably is. Have you heard this saying before? My parents said this to me before I was old enough to watch t.v. They knew that I was an impressionable young person who could be easily swayed by some sales pitch into believing that I needed the newest and best whatever they were selling. In the world in which we live, we treat this statement as truth. If something seems too good to be true, then it most likely is.

Unfortunately, for the world in which we live, this statement is often more truthful than it is not.

However, when we encounter God's promises, they will always seem to be better than what we could imagine. This can lead us to believe that his promises are simply that: too good to be true. I personally have struggled with this and still sometimes do. How can his promises actually be true when it seems too good to be true? This is never the case when it comes to God's promises, though they may be perceived in some ways as too good, they are never too good to be true.

The way we view his promises has a massive implication in this relationship goal. If we believe that they are too good to be true, then we won't be able to walk in the promise and relationship that God wants us to have with him.

This is precisely how Abraham felt when he was given his promise. This promise is found in Genesis 12.

> "The LORD said to Abram, "Go from your
> country, your people and your father's
> household to the land I will show you. "I
> will make you into a great nation, and I
> will bless you; I will make your name
> great, and you will be a blessing. I will

bless those who bless you, and whoever
curses you I will curse; and all peoples
on the earth will be blessed through
you. " [69]

While we might be in awe of this promise to Abraham, we may miss the fact that this promise would have seemed too good to be true for him. At the time the promise was given to him, Abraham was seventy-five years old and had no children. Can you imagine the shock on Abraham's face when he heard that he was going to be the father of a great nation?

This promise definitely sounded too good to be true! There was no way that God could come through on his promise to make him a great nation. Or was there...

The saying "if something is too good to be true, then it probably is" teaches nothing about trust. In fact, what it promotes is that we should not trust anything that seems or sounds too good.

Abraham trusted in God and in his promises to him despite them seeming too good to be true. This is exactly the truth that we need to hear when we think about God's promises. God's promises are going to be greater than we have ever imagined, but we cannot allow what the world has taught us about distrust to influence the way we walk into God's promises.

Understanding Covenant

God has designed his promises around a covenant. For most of us when we see the word covenant, we have no clue what that means. What is a covenant? A covenant is more than a business agreement or some sort of contract. It signifies a deep relationship that exists between two parties of a covenant, in effect, bonding two people together in friend-ship, almost like a marriage.[70]

Though the term is old, people still make covenants today. When college students sign a lease agreement, that is a covenant. When people get married to one another, that is a covenant. When we sign a contract for a new job or a loan, both are covenants.

These are all similar to covenants made back in biblical times, but they aren't identical. The biblical covenants have elements of promise within them. They are established through God's divine sanction. That means that the founda-tion of the promises are not based on the promises by equal parties. They are built on the foundation of the divine promise of God. [71] This is the essential difference between the promises we make with people on Earth: there is a divine aspect to the promises that come from God.

The covenantal promises that God has given to his people is directly tied to our relationship with him. Promises are an essential part of who God is. His promises teach us how to walk in relationship with him. God's promises are designed to lead us closer to him as the promise-maker.

There are times where we miss this relational aspect when it comes to God's promises. There is almost always a tempta-tion to make the promise more important than the promise-giver. We see Abraham facing this temptation in his relation-ship with God.

After Abraham's son was born, God asked Abraham to sacrifice his son who was the culmination of God's promise to him. Abraham was willing to adhere to the commandment of God and proceeded as directed. However, God inter-vened, and Abraham didn't end up having to sacrifice his son, because God provided an offering to take his place.[72] God's direction was a test to see where Abraham's heart was. Did he love the promise more than God who gave the promise?

There is almost always a point in every promise where we are asked to sacrifice what God has given us as a test, to make sure that the promise has not become greater than the promise-giver.

God's covenants were never meant to be broken. However, in most cases, we haven't held up our end of the deal. Thankfully, we have God's grace and mercy to cover us in our relationship with God. His grace holds us close to him even when we make mistakes. Learning how to walk in relationship with him is a process. We need his grace to maintain our relationship with him.

This doesn't mean that there won't be consequences for our wrong or bad decisions. When we break the stipulations of the promise that God has given us, there will inevitably be consequences. Abraham faced the consequences when he tried to speed up God's promise that he was given. The Israelites also learned this as they faced the consequences of their decision to walk away from the covenantal boundaries that God had set for them.

The presence of consequences does not mean that there is an absence of God's grace. While grace in these moments may seem like it is fleeting, I promise you the consequence you may face is wrapped in an excess amount of grace as we learn to walk in God's promises.

The Point Of Promises

The point of promises in our lives is not only to develop a deeply intimate relationship with Jesus but also to point to Jesus. Jesus is the culmination of all promises; he is the end and the beginning. It is all about Jesus.

> *"For no matter how many promises God has*
> *made, they are "Yes" in Christ. And so*
> *through him the "Amen" is spoken by us to*
> *the glory of God."*[73]

Every promise is yes and Amen in Christ. This is a fantastic promise in itself. However, this promise does not give us the liberty to begin to pick and choose which promises we want. When we try to cherry-pick his promises, we start trying to be our own God.

Christianity is not a promise buffet; it's not a lineup of items where we are given the option to say yes to some and no to others, depending on our mood, our interest, or our inclination. Christianity is equally abundant and overflowing with goodness, but that does not give us the liberty to do what we want with God's promises.

The provision that God provides is also not the purpose of promises. The provision that we receive while walking in his promise sustains us, but it also points to the one who provides. That is the entire point of provision. It is intended to point us to the provider.

When we receive a gift from someone we don't thank the gift for giving it to us, do we? Can you imagine holding a present on your birthday and thanking the gift itself for being so generous? No, of course, we turn to thank the person who has given it to us.

Let's take this concept one step farther.

Take a look at the things that have been given to you this past Christmas. Or maybe for your last birthday. I would bet that the majority of us can name the person who gave a gift to us, but can you remember everything you were given? Probably not. The point is that the gifts we receive are given to make you think of the gift-giver. That is the purpose of why

God provides in our lives. Not only do we need it to live and thrive, but it also points us to the one who provided it.

While walking in God's promises, we often see God's provision in amazing ways. God will provide us with what we need to walk into the promise. We sometimes mistake this provision for something it is not. We believe God has provided in our lives just because he can. His provision is only one part of the bigger picture that God has in mind for us.

We can also make the mistake of seeking the provision rather than seeking the one who gives the provision. Remember that the point of promises is God himself. He is the end-goal and the best part of the promise that we can receive. However, in the moments where we are in desperate need, it can be difficult for us to remember that promises are ultimately about God.

We would do well to remember the words of Jesus, that the goal is to seek his kingdom and his righteousness and then all these things will be added unto you.[74]

The point of Jesus' words is for us to raise our eyes to the point of what we are supposed to be seeking. Him. In the midst of our need, Jesus says to not worry about other things, but to seek the kingdom of God and through him, we will be provided for, cared for, and loved. When we seek the kingdom first, the provision we need will then be given to us.

We also need to be sure that we don't fall into the belief that God has no concern for our everyday needs. While Jesus is telling us to seek the Kingdom of God and not to worry about the other things we may begin to think that he is not concerned with small things. That couldn't be farther from the truth. God has a sincere desire to meet our every need.

Herein lies the beauty of Jesus, in the midst of our deepest need he has already provided what we need through his sacrifice on the cross. If Jesus has already met our deepest need, then we can trust him to provide whatever else we need, as well.

The Process

When we are given promises, they almost never immediately come to fruition. While there are a few exceptions to this, God has designed it this way to draw us into a deeper relationship with him. This takes time. This time in between when the promise is given and when the promise comes to fruition is what I call the process.

Every promise has a process. When God gives his people a promise, there is always a behind-the-scenes process that has to occur for them to walk into the promise that he had given them. Every step that we go through prepares us and guides us towards walking into the promise that God gives. The only way we see God's promise come to fruition is if we are willing to go through his process for our life.

We get a picture into Abraham's process towards God's promise in Genesis 12:4-19:18.

To walk into the promise that God has given us, we must walk in obedience to the process that God has for our journey. One of the first steps in Abraham's process involved God's command to leave his home and relocate his family to the place where God called him to go. Without question, he and his family moved.[75] Abraham had an uncontainable desire to walk in what God had for him and his family. Through each step of obedience in the process, Abraham's desire for a relationship with God grew. In fact, we see that Abraham's obedience in the process led to a deeper intimacy with God.

Abraham's total trust in God was nothing short of incredible. He is a model for us all on how to fully trust God in the process. He not only had trust in who God was, but he was willing to comply with what God said, too.

Even though for a majority of the time we see Abraham trusting in God promise, we also see him falling into the temptation of trying to make shortcuts during the process. After years of walking in the process and not seeing the promise come to fruition, Abraham chose to take matters into his own hands. He wished to make the promise happen in his own strength and his own timing.

Abraham slept with a woman who was not his wife to make God's promise happen. Abraham's wife, Sarah, was convinced that she would never bear children and encouraged him to do this. Abraham didn't necessarily do so with a heart of frustration or resentment. I believe that he wished to be faithful to the promise of God and chose to pursue it this way. He did so because he was swayed by the people around him who encouraged him to stray from God's word.

His story is a good reminder that we cannot speed up God's process, but also cannot allow others to influence our walk with God in a negative way. There will be people who tell you that you may be in the wrong place with God. They will try to convince you to make what God told you happen differently. God's Word, his promises, are faithful and true. We can no more edit God's promises to us than we can change the direction of our lives without deviating from God's plan. And we should not be convinced by others who tell us differently.

Through this process, God's character is revealed, as he provides for our needs in the life that he has designed for us. What we can learn through this process, is our deep-seated need for a relationship with God. God will always provide for us in mighty ways, teaching us that we are in need of him.

Fulfilled Promises

In Genesis 21 we see the promise of God beginning to materialize in Abraham's life. The fulfillment of God's promise was initiated by the birth of his son, Isaac. His wife Sarah bore this son, in which a nation was going to be birthed through. It was twenty-five years before Abraham saw the promise come to fruition. Twenty-five years of walking in the process prepared Abraham for the outcome of God's promise. Years of growing in trust, love, and knowledge of who God is, happened in the process.

However, God isn't finished with us when we have started to walk into the promise he has given us. God's relationship with Abraham was not over when the promise was seen in the birth of his son.

We are able to see how God walked with Abraham through the beginning of the promise until his life was over on this earth. Abraham set an excellent example for us that the outcome of a promise is not a destination but a lifestyle. Abraham lived in and through the promise that God gave him. It was a continuation of growing in relationship with God.

There will be times when we walk into the fulfillment of the promise that God has given us and will be tempted to believe that his promises haven't come true. God's promise to Abraham was that he was going to be the father of a nation. Yet Abraham had only one son who was going to be the foundation of the entire nation of Israel. One son was the outcome of God's promise to Abraham in his lifetime.

We shouldn't doubt God's promises to us even when those promises don't seem to line up precisely with what we had initially thought. Like Abraham, many people would also believe that one would need many children to be the father of a nation.

Could God grow an entire nation out of one child?

God's promise to Abraham was not seen fully until much later. Hundreds of years after him moving, the nation that was from the line of Abraham walked into the land that God had promised him.[76]

For us, there will undoubtedly be promises that come into our lives, promises we may not see come to fruition and promises meant for the generations to come. We may never fully realize the entirety of the promise in our lives, but we are still invited to walk into the promise that God has given us.

The life Abraham lived throughout the process and the outcome of God's promise, is an excellent example for us all. Despite his fallout with his wife's servant, Abraham exemplified what it meant to walk out God's design for a relationship with him. This love, faith, and trust in God has been and continues to be inspiring to generations after him.

Hopefully, by now, you can see that God is inviting you to walk into his promises. There are so many promises found in scripture that it is almost mind-numbing! However, as we have discussed, Christianity isn't a promise buffet. We cannot pick and choose which promise we want and when we want it. Promises come divinely through God's perfect timing in our lives. Promises are an amazing gift that God gives us, and we must walk in humility, thankfulness, and patience as he works them out, in, and through our lives.

I want to encourage you to work through the promises God gave his people by reading and understanding them throughout scripture. Look at how he has promised something and worked through the stages of a relationship with them. What was he teaching them? How were they responding to his prompting? Dig through these truths. The better we understand how God uses promises, the clearer we will understand how he will use them in our own lives.

What are his promises to you?

13

YOUR FIRST RELATIONSHIP GOAL

I hope as you've read the pages of this book you have encountered God's desire for a relationship with you. However, it isn't just enough to read about his desire. He wants you to walk in it.

This chapter is specifically designed to help you navigate your first relationship goal with God! This is not a simple 10-minute exercise that should be skimmed over. This chapter was developed to help you begin a lifestyle of walking in a deepening relationship with God.

There are so many relationship goals that we can have with God that it may seem overwhelming at first. However, God doesn't want to leave us overwhelmed with no place to begin to walk into a deeper relationship with him. He will help lead you into your first relationship goal through the power of the Holy Spirit.

Before we begin, I want to give you a few helpful tips to get the most out of this chapter. First, it is beneficial to go to a place that is quiet, and where there will be no distractions. Then you should turn off all of your electronic devices to avoid any further distractions. Next, if you are having a difficult time hearing God while answering these questions ask him if there is a reason you can't hear him. You may experience as you are working through this chapter that God may not speak to you right away. It may take time, so be willing to wait on the Lord.

Just as Moses recorded the stages of the Israelites journey in Numbers 33, I believe that you can and should begin to write down how God moves in your life as you journey with him as well.

The following questions aren't the only questions that may need to be asked, so don't be afraid to go further than the questions I have provided here. This chapter is designed just to get you started on the journey towards walking in your first relationship goal with God. You may run completely out of room in this book as you begin, and I pray that your journey with God would go well beyond the pages that follow.

The first step is to pray through the relationship goals that we discussed in this book. As you pray, ask God if there is a certain one that he wants to begin with you now. (**Write down what God speaks to you in the blank spaces that follow each question.**)

After you know which relationship goal he has given you, ask God to continue to describe what he desires your relationship to look like. Are there any specifics about the relationship goal he wants to share with you?

The next step is to ask God if there are things from your past that are hindering you from walking into this relationship goal. If there are, then ask God to help you work through these hindrances.

Now begin to ask what this relationship goal reveals about God? Are any of your views of God being challenged by this relationship goal?

Finally, ask God what this relationship goal reveals about who he created you to be. Is there something that needs to change because of this?

NOTES

Introduction

1. A. W. Tozer, *God's Pursuit of Man,* (Chicago, IL: Moody Publishers, 2015), 15.

Chapter One: God's Desire

2. Luke 19:10 (NIV)

3. Romans 5:8 (NIV)

4. Revelation 21:3 (NIV)

5. Genesis 5:22-24 (NIV)

6. Hebrews 11:5 (NIV)

Chapter Two: God's Design

7. Exodus 13:21 (NIV)

8. Ecclesiastes 3:1-8 (NIV)

9. Exodus 33:15 (NIV)

10. Exodus 14:2-3 (NIV)

11. John 16:33 (NIV)

12. Deuteronomy 31:6 (NIV)

13. Exodus 13:17-18 (NIV)

14. Numbers 14:34 (NIV)

Chapter Three: The Struggle Is Real

15. Genesis 2:16,17 (NIV)
16. Genesis 3:6 (NIV)
17. Genesis 3:21 (NIV)
18. Revelation 13:8 (NIV)
19. Romans 3:23 (NIV)
20. Ephesians 2:8-9 (NIV)
21. Luke 10:20 (NIV)
22. Galatians 1:6-7 (NIV)
23. Galatians 2:21 (NIV)

Chapter Four: The Holy Spirit's Role

24. John 16:7 (NIV)
25. Ephesians 5:18 (NLT)
26. 1 Thessalonians 5:19 (NIV)
27. 1 Timothy 4:14 (NIV)
28. Galatians 5:22-23 (NIV)
29. Ephesians 6:18 (NIV)
30. John 16:13 (NIV)
31. John 14:26 (KJV)
32. Philippians 4:7 (NIV)

Chapter Five: Friendship

33. John 15:16 (NIV)
34. John 15:13 (NIV)
35. 2 Chronicles 20:7 (NIV), Isaiah 41:8 (NIV), James 2:23 (NIV)
36. Exodus 33:11 (NIV)

Chapter Six: Fatherhood

37. John 14:9 (NIV)
38. Romans 8:14-17 (NIV)

39. Matthew 7:9-11 (NIV)

40. Luke 3:22 (NIV)

41. Psalm 68:5 (NIV)

Chapter Seven: Marriage

42. Hosea 3:1 (NIV)

43. 2 Timothy 2:13 (NIV)

Chapter Eight: Lord and King

44. Matthew 2:9-11 (NIV)

45. John 18:33-37 (NIV)

46. 1 Samuel 8:6-8 (NIV)

47. 1 Samuel 8:10 (NIV)

48. Matthew 20:25-28 (NIV)

49. Matthew 7:21-23 (NIV)

50. Mark L. Strauss, *Four Portraits, One Jesus: A Survey of Jesus and the Gospels,* (Grand Rapids, MI: Zondervan, 2007), 487.

51. Mark 10:23 (NIV)

Chapter Nine: Shepherd

52. Isaiah 40:11 (NIV)

53. W. Phillip Keller, *A Shepherd Looks at Psalm 23,* (Grand Rapids, MI: 2007*), 21.*

54. Isaiah 53:6 (NIV)

55. John 10:3-4 (NIV)

56. John 10:5 (NIV)

57. Psalm 23:1 (NIV)

Chapter Ten: Rabbi

58. Joseph M. Stowell, *Following Christ,* (Grand Rapids, MI: Zondervan, 1996), 65.

59. John 1:45-49 (NIV)

60. John 1:49 (NIV)

61. Luke 14:25-33 (NIV)

62. Ann Spangler and Lois Tverberg, *Sitting at the Feet of Rabbi Jesus,* (Grand Rapids, MI: Zondervan, 2009), 51.

63. Shemuel Safari and Menahem Stern, eds., *The Jewish People in the First Century,* (Amsterdam: Van Gorcum, 1976), 964.

64. Ann Spangler and Lois Tverberg, *Sitting at the Feet of Rabbi Jesus,* (Grand Rapids, MI: Zondervan, 2009), 33-34.

65. Mark 1:21-22 (NIV)

66. John 7:14-16 (NIV)

Chapter Eleven: God's Promises

67. Genesis 12:2 (NIV)

68. Isaiah 55:11 (NIV)

69. Genesis 12:1-3 (NIV)

70. Ann Spangler and Lois Tverberg, *Sitting at the Feet of Rabbi Jesus,* (Grand Rapids, MI: Zondervan, 2009), 133.

71. R. C. Sproul, *The Promises of God: Discovering The One Who Keeps His Word,* (Colorado Springs, CO: David C. Cook, 2013), 11.

72. Genesis 22:11-13 (NIV)

73. 2 Corinthians 1:20 (NIV)

74. Matthew 6:33 (NIV)

75. Genesis 12:4 (NIV)

76. Joshua 3:14-17 (NIV)

ACKNOWLEDGMENTS

This book wouldn't have been a reality without my wife's love and encouragement over the past couple of years as I have tried to put it in words. Talia, you are one of a kind, and I can't thank you enough! To my family, your prayer and support over my life has set the foundation of the ministry that I am doing. To my editor, Crystal, thank you for all of your kind words and support throughout this process. You made this book what it is today. Cass you rock! Your words at times were exactly what I needed to continue moving forward. I can't thank my cover designer Jacob enough, either. Thank you for your patience and dedication to see this through. To everyone else who has supported me throughout this entire process, I can't thank you all enough.

ABOUT THE AUTHOR

Garrett lives in Kansas along with his wife, Talia. He's a graduate of Fort Hays State University and has a master's degree in Applied Biblical Studies from Moody Bible Institute. Garrett formerly worked as the Assistant Director for *Encounter*, a growing and vibrant young adult ministry in Hays, Kansas. He now works with Forge, a parachurch organization, and travels as an itinerant preacher speaking to people in the United States and around the world.

Interested in booking Garrett for an event? Check out his sermons and book him for your next event online!
https://forgeforward.org/speakers/garrett-kahrs/

CPSIA information can be obtained
at www.ICGtesting.com
Printed in the USA
FSHW01n0323140918

9 780692 153321